The Book of Mormon: A Very Short Introduction

Very Short Introductions available now:

For more information visit our web sites
www.oup.co.uk/general/vsi/
www.oup.com/us

Terryl L. Givens

THE BOOK OF MORMON

A Very Short Introduction

OXFORD
UNIVERSITY PRESS

OXFORD
UNIVERSITY PRESS

Oxford University Press, Inc., publishes works that further
Oxford University's objective of excellence
in research, scholarship, and education.

Oxford   New York
Auckland   Cape Town   Dar es Salaam   Hong Kong   Karachi
Kuala Lumpur   Madrid   Melbourne   Mexico City   Nairobi
New Delhi   Shanghai   Taipei   Toronto

With offices in
Argentina   Austria   Brazil   Chile   Czech Republic   France   Greece
Guatemala   Hungary   Italy   Japan   Poland   Portugal   Singapore
South Korea   Switzerland   Thailand   Turkey   Ukraine   Vietnam

Copyright © 2009 Oxford University Press, Inc.

Published by Oxford University Press, Inc.
198 Madison Avenue, New York, NY 10016

www.oup.com

Oxford is a registered trademark of Oxford University Press

Library of Congress Cataloging-in-Publication Data
Givens, Terryl L.
The Book of Mormon : a very short introduction / Terryl L. Givens.
p. cm.
Includes bibliographical references and index.
ISBN 978-0-19-536931-1 (pbk.)
1. Book of Mormon—Introductions.   I. Title
BX8627.G57 2009
289.3'22—dc22
2009002656

Printed by Integrated Books International, United States of America
on acid-free paper

To Terry and Vicki, who "live after the manner of happiness."

Contents

List of Illustrations

PART I
The Book of Mormon
speaks for itself

Chapter 1
Origins, narrators, and structure

The Book of Mormon, first published in 1830 in upstate New York, is at the center of a complex tapestry of intersecting narratives, each with a very different beginning. These multicolored threads weave a story of seafaring Israelites and an American farm-boy prophet, of pre-Columbian Christians and nineteenth-century gold plates, of vanished civilizations in Central America, and the genesis of one of the world's fastest growing religions. Any attempt to distill into a plot summary a religious text as multilayered as the Book of Mormon would necessarily misrepresent its meaning and significance. But for purposes of general orientation, a synopsis of the Book of Mormon would go something like this: The Book of Mormon tells the story of an Israelite clan under the patriarch Lehi that flees Jerusalem just before the Babylonian captivity (ca. 600 BCE), sails to the Western Hemisphere, and establishes a colony. The clan immediately fractures into two opposing parties of the generally peaceful Nephites and the generally aggressive Lamanites. There follow one thousand years of fratricidal wars, missionary efforts going in both directions, and cycles of prosperity and spiritual decline.

In telling the story of the Trojan War, some poets opted to begin with the construction of the gigantic horse that heralded the final apocalypse, some with the sailing of the Achaean fleet, some with the abduction of Helen of Troy, or even her birth. One could also begin in the modern age, with Heinrich Schliemann's excavations of the city's ruins, or our modern texts of Homer, and work backward to reconstruct the city of King Priam and its eventual destruction.

In a similar way, one could begin the story of the Book of Mormon from any number of points. One could start with the middle eastern world of the sixth century BCE, in which the narrative begins. Or with the description Lehi's son Nephi gives of his commission to maintain a family history of his people after they arrive in the New World. Or working from the other direction, one could begin with the Book of Mormon's publication in March 1830, the immediate furor it created, and its role as a lightning rod for both conversion and criticism. One could begin a little earlier, with Joseph Smith's account of his recovery of buried gold plates in 1827, or with the first visit to Smith of an angel named Moroni in 1823, or with the Second Great Awakening (ca. 1790–1840) that conditioned an entire generation's religious expectations and molded the range of dreams and visions and human institutions that reflected their deepest religious yearnings.

What the Book of Mormon claims to be is so radical that the storms of controversy over its origins and authenticity have almost completely obscured the text itself. The book presents itself as a revelation from God to a boy prophet, comprising scripture equal in significance and authority to the Bible, and heralding the opening of the heavens after a silence of almost two millennia. The Bible alone excepted, the Book of Mormon is by far the most widely printed and circulated book in the history of the Western Hemisphere. Yet, the Roman Catholic scholar of Mormonism Thomas O'Dea's humorous observation is also astute: "The Book of Mormon has not been universally considered by its critics as one of those books that must be read in order to have an opinion of it." The circumstances surrounding the book's purported translation and publication have been so controversial, and the religious ramifications of belief and disbelief so profound, that relatively little attention has been paid to what the book actually says. From its publication in 1830, the text has been the contested focus of claims and counterclaims, a complex reception history involving church-building, persecution, environmental explanations, and proselytizing fury. Believers and nonbelievers alike have seen the central fact of the book's origins, as either inspired scripture or fanciful fabrication, as the most important point. In the process, the pages themselves have been rendered largely silent.

This volume will therefore go against the grain of many Book of Mormon treatments by serving, first and foremost, as an introduction to the Book of Mormon itself, by which I mean the narrative between the covers. As far as possible, I have chosen to let the record tell its own story. The focus here will be on the persons, themes, and events described by myriad authors, editors, and anonymous chroniclers from Nephi to Moroni. Only later will we turn to survey the modern history of the Book of Mormon, and the role it has played in the Church of Jesus Christ of Latter-day Saints (LDS). The narrative incorporates numerous genres, including prophecies, conversion narratives, epistles, and sermons, along with an account of political developments, intrigues, and family dramas. Above all else, however, the Book of Mormon is a collection of overlapping and intersecting stories that chronicle the role God plays in the lives of a host of individuals. These stories unfold against a backdrop of epic history, involving tribes and peoples, exodus and colonization, church-building and wars of destruction. But the focus of the Book of Mormon is always on the individual. Like the Hebrew Bible and the New Testament, the Book of Mormon attests to the sovereignty of a living God. The words of the Book of Mormon are principally personal accounts of how that living God actively intervenes in human life, answers prayers, makes and keeps covenants with individuals as well as peoples, and directs the lives of those who look to him for guidance and for knowledge. The God who emerges from these pages is a God of "tender mercies."

To those familiar with the Bible, the Book of Mormon will present a mix of the new and the known. It suggests a number of familiar themes, only to recast them with enough novelty to make of them an utterly new scripture. For example, it opens with a scene steeped in the trappings of biblical prophets and prophecy at the time of Jeremiah, then moves decisively in the direction of a divine discourse, a personal revelation, that is literal, egalitarian, and indicative of a God entirely passible, accessible, and personal in his interactions with individuals. Christ is a central figure in the Book of Mormon. It documents his Palestinian birth and life, crucifixion, and resurrection, but then explodes their sublime historical uniqueness by reenacting Christ's ministry and ascension in a New World setting, and by suggesting there were others besides. Similarly, the book affirms Jehovah's covenants with Israel, even as it specifies America as a separate "land of promise," and then chronicles a whole series of portable Zions founded and abandoned by covenant peoples in successive waves. The Book of Mormon affirms the Bible's status as scripture, even as it qualifies it. For while it testifies to "the gospel of Jesus Christ" and predicts its modern-day restoration in purity, the Book of Mormon demolishes the Bible's monopoly on its articulation. It makes the Bible one in a series of God's textual revelations to mankind. In these ways and others, the Book of Mormon occupies the unusual position of invoking and affirming Biblical concepts and motifs, even as it rewrites them in fairly dramatic ways. The book has thus unavoidably been seen by readers past and present as emulating Christian scripture in innumerable ways, even as it subverts Christian ideas about the closed nature of the Christian scriptural canon. But before it accomplishes any of these ends, the Book of Mormon is the story of God's personal and intimate dealings with flesh-and-blood characters caught up in dramas of family, rather than national, dimensions. The concrete particularity of those individuals, and the traces they leave, is the book's first concern.

The Book of Mormon opens with a series of sentences that claim and reaffirm one central point: the original story that we are reading was personally narrated by a historical character, Nephi the son of Lehi: "I Nephi... make a record of my proceedings in my days;" he writes. Then adds, "I make a record in the language of my father," "I make" a record which I know "is true," "I make it with my own hand," and "I make it according to my knowledge."

Why this redundancy? Why such emphatic insistence on the literal origins of the record at Nephi's own hand? Clearly, this is unlike the impersonal voice with which Genesis opens the biblical account of creation, and which focuses on cosmic history, epic events, and God's primal acts of creation, with its portentous, "In the beginning, God created..." By contrast, the Book of Mormon's first named author urgently presses upon his audience the very human, very local, and very historical nature of his narrative. It is as far removed from mythic beginnings and anonymous narratives as he can possibly make it. This is firsthand, eyewitness history of local events. It is a beginning also strikingly unlike the gospels of the New Testament. The anonymity of those books attributed to Matthew, Mark, Luke, and John seems calculated to emphasize the infinitely greater significance of the Christ who is the focus of their narratives. The authors disappear in deference to the Messiah they proclaim. The Book of Mormon, by contrast, begins with the personal introduction of the book's first author.

Before turning to the story he tells, we need to consider how this theme of personal authorship is developed, since it constitutes a core of the scripture's essential meaning. Nephi is a record-keeper who believes God has called him to maintain his clan's history. He at some point awakens to the significance of his record, and the fact that it has a role to play in the future of his people. (Nephi learns in vision that his "seed" will write things of importance to future generations of gentiles [1 Ne. 13:35; see also 2 Ne. 3:12]). Nephi is of course unable personally to steer and shepherd his work to this eventual audience that he only vaguely apprehends, and his focus remains on his immediate family and posterity. His preoccupation with audience, and with self-authentication in the face of his inability to control the fate of his written words and the terms of their reception, weighs upon him like a sacred burden. Hence, the motif that Nephi emphatically foregrounds is the question of provenance.

In art history, provenance means derivation. More fully, it means authenticity that is secured in a particular way, by establishing the unbroken history of transmission of an object from original owner to the present. In the Book of Mormon, as we shall see, we never lose sight of the transmission chain. There is a remarkable consistency to this aspect of the Book of Mormon; at the same time, these authors and editors show marked awareness of an audience that shifts dramatically in the course of the narrative.

Nephi will faithfully maintain not just one, but two parallel accounts of his people (one of which is no longer extant in any form, as we will see later). He tells us he begins writing his first record about eleven years after the flight from Jerusalem, in what would be about 589 BCE by the Book of Mormon's reckoning, in obedience to a specific command of the Lord (1 Ne. 19:1). This record, we learn, is largely a family history, recounting the significant events and developments pertaining to his father's family in the Old World and the family's establishment and development in the New. It is, essentially, a historical chronicle of his clan. In response to another divine directive, twenty years later he commences a second, more religiously oriented account and maintains it until 544 BCE. This is the account that fills the first 117 pages of text in the modern edition, making Nephi by far the major author of the Book of Mormon (though much of his material is explicitly borrowed from Isaiah). He gives in these pages an outline of his family's exodus from Jerusalem, voyage to a promised land, and dispersal into two rival factions of Nephites (those aligned with himself) and Lamanites (those aligned with his rebellious brother Laman). His brother Jacob describes his commission from Nephi to continue the record-keeping ("Nephi gave me, Jacob, a commandment ... that I should preserve these plates and hand

8

them down unto my seed, from generation to generation"—Jac. 1:1–3), and does so for an indeterminate period. He concludes his portion of the record by clearly stating the passing on of the commission to his son Enos ("I told him the things which my brother Nephi had commanded me, and he promised obedience unto the commands"—Jac. 7:27). Enos likewise assumes stewardship for the duration of his life.

We see the preoccupation of Nephi echoed in the pattern that pervades the balance of the Book of Mormon. Each inheritor of the plates attests to the unbroken chain of transmission and calls the responsibility to continue the tradition a "commandment" passed on through the generations. The weight of solemn obligation felt by these chroniclers is evident in their clear attestations of a responsibility both executed and then transferred, and explains one of the more curious features of the Book of Mormon's structure, which is the series of minibooks that follow upon the heels of Enos's record. The records of Nephi, Jacob, and Enos are progressively shorter, and that of Enos's son Jarom is only two pages, making it the shortest of all books named for their authors. (The only exception is the Words of Mormon, but that is more of an explanatory editorial insertion than a chapter proper.) Following Jarom's brief account, however, the succeeding chronicles are too short to constitute books. In one case, that of Chemish, his stewardship takes the form of a single paragraph. But this very brevity, together with the self-confessed wickedness of some of the authors, serves only to reinforce more dramatically the efficacy of the imposed obligation to maintain intact the line of transmission, the authentication of the provenance, of the sacred records. This is the message conveyed loudly and clearly by the economical Chemish: "Now I, Chemish, write what few things I write in the same book with my brother; for behold, I saw the last which he wrote, that he wrote it with his own hand; and he wrote it in the day that he delivered them unto me. And after this manner we keep the records, for it is according to the commandments of our fathers. And I make an end" (Omni 9). These brief first-person

9

accounts continue a few more pages until an abrupt editorial intrusion that complicates our picture of the record we are reading.

Mormon, a prophet and record-keeper writing in the fourth century CE, explains that he is the editor and compiler of a master narrative of which the portions we have been reading, authored by Nephi, are a self-contained, unabridged part. But virtually all that follows in the Book of Mormon has been subjected to Mormon's abridging hand. With apparent redundancy, he also edited and included Nephi's second, parallel history, but that is not a part of the modern Book of Mormon, having been lost before publication in 1830. Providentially, as it were, the second, spiritual record of Nephi survived to fill the void left by loss of the first account. What this means is that the Book of Mormon in its modern form

Who Kept the Records in the Book of Mormon?

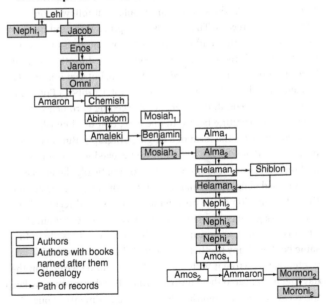

1. **Book of Mormon Authors**

comprises the unabridged writings of Nephi and his descendents, covering a period from 600 BCE until about 130 BCE. They record what they consider to be "precious things" of spiritual worth to Nephi and his people. In 130 BCE, Mormon informs us, the line of record-keepers having died out, Chemish's son Amaleki hands the plates over to the secular ruler of his day, King Benjamin. The particular details of subsequent transmission history are collapsed into Mormon's assertion that, from this point on, we will be reading his abridgment of a secular history of his people, one that is maintained for several hundred subsequent years. The theme of certain provenance is reaffirmed, as Mormon tells us he has duly inherited the records of his people and personally carried out their abridgment.

All this complicates the structure of the narrative considerably. Following Nephi's history, we have a good deal of third-person narration of wars and political developments, interspersed with first-hand accounts, numerous epistles, descriptions and apparent transcripts of sermons and missionary experiences (suggesting either that the sacred and secular histories have merged in the chronicles, or that Mormon is availing himself of both), editorial asides, and near the end of the compilation, Moroni's abridgment (the Book of Ether) of an entirely distinct record describing the rise and fall of a civilization of "Jaredites" dating from the time of the Tower of Babel. The abrupt transition from Nephi to Mormon ushers in a dramatic change of authorial perspective, tone, and thematic preoccupations. Nephi, remember, is writing at the beginning of what he sees prophetically as a minor colony with an important destiny in the land of promise. Mormon, on the other hand, is editing his history from the other side of time, having personally witnessed the collapse into depravity and barbarism, and eventual genocide, of his own people. His son Moroni, in a pattern now a thousand years old, testifies that he has resumed the record-keeping of his fallen father. And then he tells us that he is sealing up the records, bringing to closure a book of scripture whose narrative framing constitutes a sacred genealogy, but not of Christ back to Abraham or of the human family back to Adam. It attests rather to its own provenance, in a chain of authority traceable from God's first command to Nephi, through a thousand years of providential history, to the plates' earthly tomb. In this sense, the Book of Mormon serves more as a sacred relic than a mere repository. The narrative thread it embodies stretches back unbroken through centuries of obscurity and silence to its origins in a world pervaded by contact with the miraculous and the divine.

Book of Mormon Plates and Records

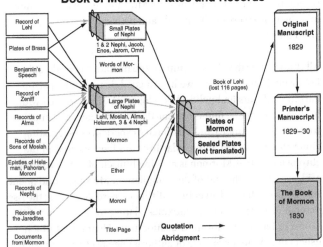

2. **Structure of Book of Mormon**

Chapter 2
Themes

What is Nephi's place and moment in time, which he asserts so emphatically? The city of Jerusalem, he tells us, at the very beginning of the first year of the reign of Zedekiah (roughly 600 BCE). This information anchors the narrative in secular history, even as it establishes the first of many interconnections with biblical history and texts. (This date becomes one of three temporal reference points that orient and ground all subsequent history in the Book of Mormon. The other two will be the inauguration of a government based on reigning judges, at around 91 BCE, and the birth of Jesus Christ.) It is a moment of acute national crisis for Judah. A few years earlier, the reforming king Josiah had died in battle against Egypt, which then made Judah its vassal. After Egypt's subsequent defeat at Carchemish by Babylon in 605 BCE, the Babylonians attacked Jerusalem, took thousands captive, and made the small kingdom its vassal, installing Josiah's son Jehoiakim as puppet king. In spite of the outspoken warnings of the prophet Jeremiah, Jehoiakim attempted to defect to Egypt, incurring reprisals from Babylon. After he died in 597, his son Jehoiachin served only three months before Nebuchadnezzar, ruler of Babylon, installed another of Josiah's sons, Mattaniah, renaming him Zedekiah.

The authors of the biblical books of Kings and Chronicles describe the undeviating descent of Judah from the pinnacle of righteousness under good king Josiah into increasing spiritual wickedness under subsequent rulers, culminating in open hostility between the prophet Jeremiah and the royal house. As Zedekiah assumes the throne, his choice of loyalty or rebellion, political as well as spiritual, will decide Judah's fate. This is the scene when Nephi opens the curtain on his narrative, writing that "in that same year there came many prophets, prophesying unto the people that they must repent, or the great city Jerusalem must be destroyed" (1 Ne. 1:4).

This pluralism of prophets and prophecy becomes one of the most significant features of the world that Nephi sets about chronicling. This is evident in the very next sentence, when Nephi's own father, Lehi, who emerges as one of these "many prophets," experiences the first of six visions and revelations that Nephi records. Because these visions introduce several principal themes that will occupy the Book of Mormon from its first page to its last, we will consider how they are introduced, and then examine each individually.

Six visions

We know virtually nothing for certain of Lehi or his background except that he is a person of wealth and, as his wife laments and Lehi agrees, is a "visionary man." His first recorded vision occurs as Lehi is praying "with all his heart" on behalf of his people. Strangely, this is the only one of Lehi's visions about whose content we are told nothing at all. Nephi simply reveals that as Lehi prays, "there came a pillar of fire . . . and he saw and heard much." No details of the vision, no particulars of any message, are available to distract from the fact of the visitation itself, given to a man who shares neither the public prestige nor, so far as we can tell, the national stewardship of his contemporary Jeremiah. What we do have is the sheer fact of a personal revelation, apparently containing images and words ("he saw and heard much"), that comes as a result of petitionary prayer and profoundly affects the recipient. This definition of revelation as propositional, or content-bearing, will become one of the dominant themes of the Book of Mormon, even as it is manifested in the lives of a broadening range of recipients.

Immediately following Lehi's first vision, he returns to his home and experiences a second vision. This one takes the form initially of a theophany, or vision of God, and calls to mind the divine assembly described in Old Testament passages like Psalm 82 or 2 Chronicles 18. Lehi sees "God sitting upon his throne, surrounded with numberless concourses of angels in the attitude of singing and praising their God." Then follows a sight that is decidedly without Old Testament precedent: "And it came to pass that he saw One descending out of the midst of heaven, and he beheld that his luster was above that of the sun at noon-day. And he saw also twelve others following him, and their brightness did exceed that of the stars in the firmament" (1 Ne. 1:8–10). Christians have not shrunk from reading messianic prophecies into the psalms or passages from Isaiah and Zechariah. But nothing biblical approaches the degree of specificity with which Book of Mormon prophets and writers detail their anticipation of a Christ, six centuries before his birth. Christocentrism pervades the entire text.

Following this vision, which includes foreshadowings of the destruction of Jerusalem, Lehi preaches repentance to an unreceptive populace. Like Jeremiah's exhortations, which led to his persecution and imprisonment, Lehi's public warnings prompt threats against his life. Consequently, Lehi receives a third vision, wherein God commands him to take his family and flee into the wilderness. Lehi promptly complies, setting in motion the principal action of the early Book of Mormon, the family's journey to and settlement of a new world. This exodus also establishes a structural motif, as the first of many hegiras the Book of Mormon records. Flight from the old Jerusalem and building new ones, scattering and gathering, covenantal integrity in the midst of apostasy and dispersion and a "land of promise"—all these constitute variants of the Book of Mormon's recurring theme of building Zion in the wilderness.

After a journey of three days, Lehi and his family make camp. There, in the wilderness south of Jerusalem, Lehi has a fourth dream-vision, in which he is commanded to send his four sons back to Jerusalem to secure a record of the Jews together with a family genealogy, inscribed on plates of brass. This is a formidable challenge because the plates are in the possession of one Laban, apparently a Jewish official of some standing. Twice the brothers fail, almost losing their lives in the process. Nephi himself returns a third time and succeeds unaided, but only through the extreme measure of killing a drunken and helpless Laban at the persistent urging of "the Spirit." The cost in expense, effort, and human life demonstrates and justifies a profound valuation of scripture—a concept that comes to be developed in the Book of Mormon in ways very unlike Catholic and Protestant notions.

Once in possession of the brass plates, Lehi relates yet another divine mandate he has received, this time sending his sons on a quest presumably more to their liking: obtaining wives. If they had harbored doubts about the duration or remoteness of their exile, the command to acquire companions before continuing must have told them that their flight was a definitive exile. Lehi's sons and daughters need companions if the band of refugees is to have a sustainable future. Or in Lehi's words, "his sons should take daughters to wife, that they might raise up seed unto the Lord." This concern with family and posterity, and the fervent hope that descendents will prosper in the face of contention, schism, and eventual civil war, reinforce this narrative's essential identity as a clan history. Like the patriarchal narratives of Genesis, the Book of Mormon, in its initial self-conceiving especially, is an epic family drama.

Nephi describes one more vision Lehi experienced shortly after the return of the sons bringing the family of Ishmael with their prospective brides (and presumably grooms). By far the most extensive of his chronicled visions, and the most memorable in the Book of Mormon, this one culminates and subsumes the long chain of heavenly revelations already recorded. The central image in his vision is a tree with resplendent white fruit, "desirable to make one happy." Other features of the allegorical dream include a large and spacious building, a rod of iron, a spacious field and a fountain of waters, Lehi's family, and multitudes of people. But now, in the pages following Lehi's description of his dream, the narrative takes a peculiar and momentous shift. For Nephi records for the first time that in the aftermath of his father's vision, he goes to the Lord in prayer, desiring that he may also "behold the things which [his] father saw" (1 Ne. 11:3).

The Spirit of the Lord appears to him, and at first leaves him in doubt as to the propriety of his request. Does he not believe his father's account? Why then ask for his own version? Assured by Nephi that he does indeed trust the words of his father, the prophet and patriarch Lehi, the Spirit breaks into a hosanna shout and blesses Nephi for seeking his personal revelatory experience. Nephi then records his version of the vision, which exceeds his father's in points of detail. It is thus by virtue of the repetition of Lehi's final vision through his son Nephi that the principal themes already outlined are reiterated and reconfirmed. First, the very circumstance of the vision's duplication for Nephi's benefit emphatically attests to the desirability and worthiness of the quest for personal revelation. The apparent redundancy of the vision, and its bestowal on an individual outside the channels of prophetic leadership or patriarchal direction, point to a more egalitarian, decentralized, less priestly version of revelation than is typical of Old Testament texts. Nephi summarizes this lesson, the backbone of his people's entire scriptural and religious history, when he writes that his desire "to see and hear and know" the things of God "by the power of the Holy Ghost" will be granted by God "unto all those who diligently seek him.... For he that diligently seeketh shall find; and the mysteries of God shall be unfolded unto them, as well in these times as in times of old, and as well in times of old as in times to come" (1 Ne. 10:17–19).

The Christocentrism of Nephi's vision is powerfully manifest in the answer to his question concerning the meaning of the central, commanding image of the vision, a magnificent tree with white fruit. Instead of receiving an answer in words, Nephi is shown the Virgin Mary, bearing the young Christ in her arms. He then apprehends that the fruit of the tree signifies the love of God, concretized in the gift of his son. He sees as well the Savior's ministry, his crucifixion, and in a dramatic coda to the gospel version of the passion and resurrection, Nephi also witnesses the risen Christ appearing to Nephi's future descendents in "the land of promise." Christ, then, is the governing image in this vision, the consummation of all righteous desire, and the historical culmination of the process of exile and new world building that Lehi initiates.

With that land of promise, we come again to the theme of the third vision—Zion and wilderness. The prior mention of that motif makes sense of Lehi's unusual emphasis on the temporal and geographical details of his present vision. His very first words of description referred to "a dark and dreary wilderness." A man appears proposing to guide him, but it still takes "the space of many hours in darkness" to reach a spacious field on the other side of "a dark and dreary waste." That may at first sound like a metaphorical refuge at the end of a spiritual wilderness, but Nephi's account emphasizes the literal, historical dimensions of successive promised lands and blessed eras. He details the dispensation of Christ's life and ministry, and the passing of that age into darkness; he witnesses the flourishing of his posterity, in a "land of promise" far from Jerusalem, and the eventual apostasy of that civilization, as "darkness [covers] the face of the land of promise"; he sees Christ's post-resurrection visit to the survivors,

18

and the reestablishment of yet another golden age of righteousness that lasts three generations before descending back into a night of sin; and he watches as yet another work of righteousness is established, this time referred to as Zion, and prophesied to be established among the gentiles in the latter days.

The final two themes are reintroduced in connection with the dominating image of the Tree of Life itself. In the vicinity of the tree are throngs of people—lost, wandering, or striving to reach its fruit. Shrouds of mist obscure the path, but a conspicuous rod of iron leads along the bank of a river, through the darkness, straight to the tree. Only those who cling to it are successful in their quest. The troublesome brothers ask Nephi the meaning of this iron rod and are told, "It is the word of God." The importance of scripture is depicted metaphorically here; as recounted in the Book of Mormon itself, national as well as individual spiritual survival is tied to its availability.

Finally, Lehi's vision of the Tree of Life is framed at both ends and marked internally by his parental preoccupation. "I have seen a vision," he says by way of introduction, "And behold, because of the thing which I have seen, I have reason to rejoice because of Nephi and also of Sam; ... But behold, Laman and Lemuel, I fear exceedingly because of you" (1 Ne. 8:2–4).

The reason for his fear is the scene that unfolds in the vicinity of the Tree of Life, the fruit of which Lehi samples, finding it "most sweet, above all that I ever before tasted." Finding that it "filled [his] soul with exceeding great joy," he immediately desires that his family should likewise partake. Looking around for his wife and children, he beckons to several of them, who come and share in the delicious fruit. Laman and Lemuel alone refuse to come and partake. In recounting the long and complex epiphany he has experienced, with its elements of peril and salvation, Christology, national destiny, and apocalypse, Lehi begins and ends with a reference to his parental concern for his children.

These five themes—personal revelation, Christ, varieties of Zion, new configurations of scripture, and the centrality of family— constitute the backbone of five distinct narratives that comprise the sacred record.

Personal revelation

One influential theologian has written, "God's revelation of Himself always occurs in such a way as to manifest more deeply his inaccessibility to our thought and imagination. All that we can know is the world. God is not the world.... He is Mystery." Another contemporary religious scholar, Elizabeth A. Johnson, agrees, and sees this as a dominant motif in Christian thought:

> The history of theology is replete with this truth: recall Augustine's insight that if we have understood, then what we have understood is not God; Anselm's argument that God is that than which nothing greater can be conceived; Hildegard's vision of God's glory as Living Light that blinded her sight; Aquinas's working rule that we can know that God is and what God is not but not what God is; Luther's stress on the hiddenness of God's glory in the shame of the cross; Simone Weil's conviction that there is nothing that resembles what she can conceive of when she says the word God; Sallie McFague's insistence on imaginative leaps into metaphor since no language about God is adequate and all of it is improper.

This is not the God of the Book of Mormon.

It is hard to talk about revelation *in* the Book of Mormon, without talking about the revelation *of* the Book of Mormon. We shall turn to the modern translation and publication of the Book of Mormon later. Suffice it for now to say that the process by which the Book of Mormon itself came into existence enacts and epitomizes the principle of revelation the record is at such pains to foster and promote. As we saw, the book opens upon a scene of prophets and prophecy set in a time of extreme national peril. Within pages, however, the focus shifts from the city of Jerusalem and its inhabitants to the destiny of a man named Lehi and his family who flee into the wilderness. As the focus narrows, the manifestations of divine communication, the interactions with God, and his interventions in human life, do not decrease but are multiplied. (This shift of direction, from a public prophet advocating national repentance for the sake of collective survival in the face of geopolitical crisis, to a father contending for the preservation of his sons and daughters in the wilderness, is a perfect example of the Book of Mormon's tendency to abruptly shift the ground under our feet. Time and again, we see familiar themes and motifs invoked—revelation, Christ, Zion, scripture—only to have the narrative swerve in a direction that reconfigures or reorients the thematic treatment.) "Prophecy was preeminently the privilege of the prophets," writes one scholar of the Hebrew Bible; prophecy is "exegesis of existence from a divine perspective," writes Abraham Heschel." In the Book of Mormon, this is emphatically not the case. Prophecy and revelation contract into the sphere of the quotidian, the personal, and the immediate, where they proliferate and flourish.

There are indications that the writers of the Book of Mormon intended the prevailing message of the book to be, in fact, openness to radically individualistic and literalistic conceptions of divine communication to mortals, i.e., dialogic revelation. The kind of revelation we are referring to is seen in the Old Testament most memorably in Moses' encounter with God on Mount Sinai, when it is recorded that "the LORD spake unto Moses face to face, as a man speaketh unto his friend" (Ex. 33:11, KJV), or in Abraham's prolonged exchange with God over the fate of Sodom, when they haggle over numbers like a housewife and a shopkeeper (Gen. 18). The anthropomorphism of these stories, figurative or mythical as it may be to today's readers, is certainly understood literally by the writer. "And the LORD went his way, as soon as he had left communing with Abraham: and Abraham returned unto his place," he writes, as if human language and human paradigms of interaction were perfectly adequate to describe prophetic negotiations with the divine.

The major thrust of the Book of Mormon is the elaboration of this model of revelation and its extension to lesser mortals. Nephi is no figure of prominence, but the son of a minor prophet and clan leader. Yet he matter-of-factly records, in language reminiscent of the Abraham account, how he "returned from speaking with the Lord, to the tent of [his] father" (1 Ne. 3:1). His nephew Enos makes clear that these encounters are not monologues in the wilderness but genuine dialogues, when he tells of his wrestle with the Lord, which is followed by a voice assuring him of God's blessing. There follows further petitioning of the Lord, whereupon God "covenanted with" Enos according to his desires. Such examples in the Book of Mormon could be multiplied almost endlessly. But what elevates this preoccupation from a sporadic motif to a governing theme is the way the status of revelation is tied to the destiny of the principal peoples in the narrative. Lehi's revelations, unheeded, anticipate but cannot prevent the destruction of Jerusalem. But directed to his own family, the revealed word of the Lord leads to escape and safety.

While in the wilderness, after Lehi's vision of the Tree of Life, his son Nephi receives his own personal version of the vision as well. Subsequently, he finds his brothers disputing over the interpretation of the vision. Nephi asks, "Have ye inquired of the Lord," and they respond, "We have not; for the Lord maketh no such thing known unto us." Whereupon Nephi rebukes them and likens their rejection of personal revelation to willful self-destruction (1 Ne. 15:9–11).

Shortly after the Tree of Life vision, the pattern of revelation continues as Lehi hears, once again, "the voice of the Lord" in the nighttime, urging him to continue his journey southward in the

Box 2.1

Personal revelation

> And it came to pass after I, Nephi, having heard all the words of my
> father, concerning the things which he saw in a vision, and also the
> things which he spake by the power of the Holy Ghost, which
> power he received by faith on the Son of God—and the Son of God
> was the Messiah who should come—I, Nephi, was desirous also
> that I might see, and hear, and know of these things, by the power
> of the Holy Ghost, which is the gift of God unto all those who
> diligently seek him, as well in times of old as in the time that he
> should manifest himself unto the children of men. (1 Ne. 10:17)

wilderness. The following morning, he finds a curious artifact, later
designated the Liahona, outside his tent. It functions as a kind
of compass that works according to the "faith and diligence and
heed" of its users. The instrument is thus a strange blend of
symbolism and functionality, since it actually indicates a direction
to be followed, but also demonstrates the principle that revelation
depends upon righteous conduct and that "by small means the
Lord can bring about great things" (1 Ne. 16:29). Personal
revelation oriented around the daily demands of a family's
wilderness trek now has both divine affirmation and concrete
embodiment. The analogy with Moses' exodus, which was
accompanied by fiery and cloudy pillars, is obvious, and Nephi
often invokes this Old Testament parallel. But the analogy only
underscores the discrepancy between the signs and thunderings
from Sinai that inspire and guide vast multitudes of a covenant
people, and the "small" but effective "means" that lead a father
and his family to a new home. The dramatic recontextualizing of
revelation seems very much the point: the Book of Mormon is
systemically reconstructing it into a principle with an egalitarian
application.

In southern Arabia, the clan turns eastward following the continuing admonitions of "the voice of the Lord" (1 Ne. 16:39). After eight long years (compared to the forty of Israel), they arrive in a coastal area they call Bountiful, and Nephi, not the patriarch Lehi, is summoned by the voice of the Lord to build a ship after a particular pattern shown to him. Surmounting the skepticism of his siblings, Nephi builds the ship, and after a harrowing sea journey the family reaches "the promised land." Arrived safely, they pitch tents, till the earth, and commence a new branch of civilization that will last a thousand years.

Flight from imminent destruction and captivity in Jerusalem, survival in the wilderness, guidance through a perilous ocean crossing, prosperity in the new world, even victory over dissenting Lamanites, are all effected through a continual stream of revelation given to family patriarchs and righteous sons, chief judges and Nephite kings. They even choose as "chief captains ... some one that had the spirit of revelation" (3 Ne. 3:19). When the people come dangerously close to destruction in the decades before Christ, it is because "they began to disbelieve in the spirit of prophecy and in the spirit of revelation" (Hel. 4:23). As the civilization at last spirals into its final self-destruction, from the midst of the carnage Mormon identifies a major culprit for future generations: "wo to him that shall deny the revelations of the Lord, and that shall say the Lord no longer worketh by revelation, or by prophecy" (3 Ne. 29:6). When his son Moroni remains the sole survivor of the apocalypse, he echoes the warning, part of his last testament from the dust, reproving those "who deny the revelations of God, and say that they are done away, that there are no revelations, nor prophecies ..." (Morm. 9:7). Then he turns to the same theme by way of final apostrophe to future generations, enjoining them to seek confirmation of the authenticity of the things they are reading, promising personal revelation to all who ask "with a sincere heart, with real intent, having faith in Christ."

Focus on Jesus Christ

Nowhere is the juxtaposition of the familiar and the unexpected more striking than in the place of Jesus Christ in the Book of Mormon. Many claims surrounding the Book of Mormon—its inscription on plates of gold, its delivery to Joseph Smith by an angel, its miraculous translation involving seer stones and Urim and Thummim—are remarkable to say the least. The most striking claim *within* the Book of Mormon is undoubtedly its insistence that the Jesus born in Bethlehem in the reign of Caesar Augustus was worshipped in the Western Hemisphere, by way of anticipation, as long ago as six centuries BCE. The subtitle printed on the Book of Mormon cover since 1982 ("Another Testament of Jesus Christ") is a recent development that reflects both the centrality of Jesus Christ in Latter-day Saint belief, and the church's concern to emphasize that belief in the face of public skepticism and uncertainty about its self-designation as Christian. But the gesture is no act of modern revisionism. On the title page itself, Moroni, upon concluding his ancient record, explains the second major purpose of the Book of Mormon to be "the convincing of the Jew and Gentile that JESUS is the CHRIST, the eternal GOD."

This assertion immediately invites the question: How did a group of ancient Israelites acquire exact foreknowledge of Jesus when their Jewish contemporaries had, at best, vaguely defined beliefs in some kind of future Messiah? The Book of Mormon seems in this regard a pseudepigraphal response to the tantalizing possibilities intimated by Peter, when he wrote that "the prophets . . . made careful search and inquiry, inquiring about the person or time that the Spirit of Christ within them indicated when it testified in advance of the sufferings destined for Christ and the subsequent glory" (1 Pet. 1:10–11, NSRV). The Church Father Eusebius argued that "Moses . . . was enabled by the Holy Spirit to foresee quite plainly the title Jesus" (evident, he believes, in his naming his successor Joshua—which transliterates as Jesus). Most Christians, however, see such biblical typology as inspired foreshadowings apparent only through hindsight. In the case of the Book of Mormon, by contrast, the references are clear and unobscured by allegory, symbolism, or cryptic allusion.

The first reference to Christ in the Book of Mormon is in Lehi's vision of One descending from heaven followed by twelve others. Later, the Tree of Life vision flowers into a lengthy exposition replete with detail. Nephi is told he will see "the son of God." He then sees a virgin, in the city of Nazareth, who is carried away in the Spirit, thereafter giving birth to "the Lamb of God, ... the Redeemer of the world." All the essential details of Christ's life as given in the New Testament are seen by Nephi in this vision dated by himself to the sixth century BCE. Jesus is baptized by a prophet, gathers twelve followers, heals and ministers to the sick, and is finally "lifted up and slain for the sins of the world" (1 Ne. 11:33).

As if they are aware of the improbable nature of their knowledge, Book of Mormon authors generally attribute it to special revelations. Lehi has a vision of the Christ before his family even leaves Jerusalem. In the vision, he is given a book, which "manifested plainly of the coming of a Messiah" (1 Ne. 1:9, 19). Later, he preaches the time of the Messiah's coming apparently based on an elaborate dream (1 Ne. 10:2–4). Nephi refers to the coming Messiah as Jesus Christ "according to ... the word of the angel of God" (2 Ne. 25:21). His mother's name, Mary, was likewise made known to King Benjamin "by an angel from God" (Mos. 3:2–8). The high priest Alma the Younger knows the Savior shall be born of Mary in Jerusalem, because "the spirit hath said this much unto me," (Alma 7:9), and so on. Jacob, Nephi's brother, insists that the very purpose of the record keeping is "that they may know that we knew of Christ, and we had a hope of his glory many hundred years before his coming; and not only we ourselves had a hope of his glory, but also all the holy prophets which were before us" (Jac. 4:4).

Box 2.2

Enos's wrestle with God

> And I will tell you of the wrestle which I had before God, before I received a remission of my sins. Behold, I went to hunt beasts in the forests; and the words which I had often heard my father speak concerning eternal life, and the joy of the saints, sunk deep into my heart. And my soul hungered; and I kneeled down before my Maker, and I cried unto him in mighty prayer and supplication for mine own soul; and all the day long did I cry unto him; yea, and when the night came I did still raise my voice high that it reached the heavens. And there came a voice unto me, saying: Enos, thy sins are forgiven thee, and thou shalt be blessed. And I, Enos, knew that God could not lie; wherefore, my guilt was swept away. And I said: Lord, how is it done? And he said unto me: Because of thy faith in Christ, whom thou hast never before heard nor seen. And many years pass away before he shall manifest himself in the flesh; wherefore, go to, thy faith hath made thee whole. (Enos 1:3–8)

Christology in the Book of Mormon is not an occasional intrusion, but the narrative backbone of the story, and the dramatic point of orientation. All of Book of Mormon history, in other words, pivots on the moment of Christ's coming. Its narrative centrality is emphasized by the steadfastness and travails of those who anticipate the Messianic moment, the subsequent Utopian era of those who keep the Coming and its significance in memory, and the rapid decline and degradation of those who don't. Book of Mormon prophets even establish their own chronology around his coming. Logic dictates that dating "Before Christ" can only occur from the perspective of a people living in the "annis Domini." But Nephi states and twice reaffirms that their departure from the Old World to the New occurs "six hundred years" before Christ's birth. To Enos it is reaffirmed that he is living "many years . . . before he shall manifest himself in the flesh" (Enos 1:8).

And to the prophetic Alma the Younger, even the demise of their civilization is dated in reference to that coming event: "Behold, I perceive that this very people, the Nephites, according to the spirit of revelation which is in me, in four hundred years from the time that Jesus Christ shall manifest himself unto them, shall dwindle in unbelief" (Alma 45:10).

As the time of Christ's birth nears, the chronicle records the cost as well as the reward that such anticipation brings. "Now it came to pass that there was a day set apart by the unbelievers, that all those who believed in those traditions should be put to death except the sign should come to pass, which had been given by Samuel the prophet" (3 Ne. 1:9). In a striking twist on soteriology, or salvation theology, the Book of Mormon records that anticipation of Christ's coming, if it extends to actual faith, is efficacious for salvation even before the event. Jarom teaches early on in the Book of Mormon that his people are "to look forward unto the Messiah, and believe in him to come as though he already was" (Jar. 1:11). But King Benjamin goes further, preaching that "the Lord God hath sent his holy prophets among all the children of men, to declare these things to every kindred, nation, and tongue, that thereby whosoever should believe that Christ should come, the same might receive remission of their sins, and rejoice with exceedingly great joy, *even as though he had already come among them.*" (Mos. 3:13; emphasis added).

Christ's first coming, in the Old World, was in humility and anonymity. His visitation to the Nephite people, after his resurrection in Jerusalem, anticipates his Second Coming of Christian hope in its drama, his glorious appearance, and the inauguration of a mini-millennial utopia. The New Testament records that at the crucifixion of Christ, the earth quaked and the veil in the Temple was rent. In the New World, according to the Book of Mormon, there were tempests and earthquakes that swallowed highways and obliterated cities. In the aftermath, a righteous remnant, gathering around the

The Book of Mormon

Temple Bountiful, hear a piercing, heavenly voice announce the risen Christ.

> And behold, they saw a Man descending out of heaven; and he was clothed in a white robe; and he came down and stood in the midst of them; and...he stretched forth his hand and spake unto the people, saying: Behold, I am Jesus Christ, whom the prophets testified shall come into the world....Arise and come forth unto me, that ye may thrust your hands into my side, and also that ye may feel the prints of the nails in my hands and in my feet, that ye may know that I am the God of Israel, and the God of the whole earth, and have been slain for the sins of the world. (3 Ne. 11:8–10, 12)

Box 2.3

Christ ministers to Nephite children

And it came to pass that Jesus spake unto them, and bade them arise. And they arose from the earth, and he said unto them: "Blessed are ye because of your faith. And now behold, my joy is full." And when he had said these words, he wept, and the multitude bare record of it, and he took their little children, one by one, and blessed them, and prayed unto the Father for them. And when he had done this he wept again; And he spake unto the multitude, and said unto them: "Behold your little ones." And as they looked to behold they cast their eyes towards heaven, and they saw the heavens open, and they saw angels descending out of heaven as it were in the midst of fire; and they came down and encircled those little ones about, and they were encircled about with fire; and the angels did minister unto them. And the multitude did see and hear and bear record; and they know that their record is true for they all of them did see and hear, every man for himself; and they were in number about two thousand and five hundred souls; and they did consist of men, women, and children. (3 Nephi 17:20–25)

Over a period of days, Jesus ministers to the people, delivers a discourse similar to the Sermon on the Mount, gives special power and authority to a chosen twelve, blesses Nephite children, and gives other instructions. Occupying several chapters, the account also includes Christ's promise of his Second Coming, institution of the Lord's Supper, some corrections to their record keeping, and tender accounts of his praying with and for his disciples, healing their sick, and a children's Pentecost replete with ministering angels.

One challenge confronted by the early Christian church was how to situate the gospel of Jesus Christ in relation to the teachings of a host of ancient philosophers, sages, and non-Jewish prophets. One solution was to accord to some of these predecessors a degree of inspiration that anticipated but did not equal the fullness of the gospel revealed in the apostolic age. In other words, the gospel was held to be in some fashion as ancient as Adam. St. Augustine, for example, held that "that which is called the Christian religion existed among the ancients, and never did not exist, from the beginning of the human race until Christ came in the flesh, at which time the true religion which already existed began to be called Christianity." According to this doctrine of *prisca theologia*, versions of the gospel were transmitted imperfectly to other peoples and cultures, affording even pagans a partial glimpse of gospel truth. The Book of Mormon suggests a more radical concept: Christ presents his own ministry to the Nephites as but one in a series of proliferating manifestations of his gospel and even his personal presence. Quoting but expanding upon words recorded in the Gospel of John, Jesus tells them,

> ye are they of whom I said: Other sheep I have which are not of this fold; them also must I bring, and they shall hear my voice; and there shall be one fold, and one shepherd....And verily, verily, I say unto you that I have other sheep, which are not of this land, neither of the land of Jerusalem, neither in any parts of that land round

about whither I have been to minister.... But I have received a
commandment of the Father that I shall go unto them, and that
they shall hear my voice. (3 Ne. 15:21, 16:1, 3).

Instead of a single unparalleled eruption of the divine into the
human, we have in the Book of Mormon a proliferation of
historical iterations, which collectively become the ongoing
substance rather than the shadow of God's past dealings in the
universe.

Wilderness and varieties of Zion

The central fact in the history of Israel is the exodus from Egypt
and the settling of the Promised Land. Millennia later, the
Puritans who settled America would see themselves as exiles from
the Old World, figurative Israelites who were guided to this
Promised Land to establish a spiritual Zion. The early Christian
saga involves movement from the covenant of blood extended to
a chosen tribe to the covenant of adoption, which creates a
community of believers; it changes from a gathering in real space,
centered in a literal Zion, to a spiritual gathering that constitutes
a figurative body in Christ. The Book of Mormon reenacts the
former, Jewish model, even as it presages the latter, Christian
version. For the Book of Mormon is the record of a people's
repeated quests for a land of promise, and their anxiety about their
covenantal status before God, even as it insistently repeats the
theme that "As many of the Gentiles as will repent are the covenant
people of the Lord" (2 Ne. 30:2).

Gods who hold dominion and sway by the power of love evoke a
particular kind of anxiety in their people. "We are never so
vulnerable as when we love," writes Freud, and that holds true in
relations with the divine as much as in relations with humans. The
fear of alienation, anxiety about rejection, and the terror of being
forgotten—these sentiments seem to be fully acknowledged and
mercifully addressed in God's institution of the covenant as a

compensating mechanism. There is no more pervasive and unifying theme to the Jewish scriptures than the covenant made with Abraham. It is the basis of both collective and individual identity. It is the foundation not just of a particular status vis-à-vis other peoples, but it is principally and primarily the guarantee of God's constant love. A woman may forget her nursing child, the Lord assures them through Isaiah, "yet I will not forget thee. Behold, I have graven thee upon the palms of my hands" (Isa. 49:15–16, KJV).

Only in this context does the dominant emotional tone of the Book of Mormon have a recognizable resonance. The Book of Mormon begins with an event that must have been traumatic to the principal actors in the drama: exodus. Not an exodus from bondage and wilderness exile to the land of promise, but exodus away from the land of promise, away from Jerusalem, the people of the covenant, from the Temple, and into

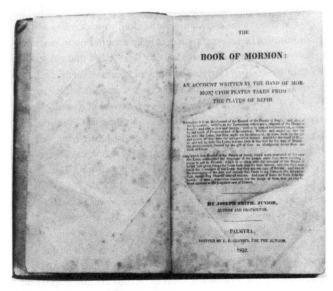

3. Book of Mormon title page, 1830

the wilderness. This is why the form of so much of Nephi's preaching, in the early days of exile, is reassurance and consolation. He invokes Isaiah repeatedly, precisely in order to convince his people that they are "a remnant of the house of Israel," and that, though broken off, they "may have hope as well as [their] brethren" (1 Ne. 19:24). A thousand years later, at the conclusion of the record, Moroni reaffirms this message by giving it pride of place on his title page. The sacred record, he writes, is "to show unto the remnant of the House of Israel what great things the Lord hath done for their fathers; and that they may know the covenants of the Lord, that they are not cast off forever."

This lesson—the portability of Zion—is reenacted so many times in the Book of Mormon story that it becomes a leitmotif. Lehi erects an altar in the wilderness and makes of his exile a sacred refuge. After a terrifying sea voyage, the clan becomes established in the promised land. But there, dissension immediately breaks out, and Nephi is directed to again flee into the wilderness and reestablish a remnant of the original remnant (2 Ne. 5). A few hundred years later, the Lord directs a subsequent king, Mosiah, to depart from there "into the wilderness" with "as many as would hearken" (Omni 1:13). Arrived in Zarahemla, Mosiah and his people encounter another remnant from Jerusalem who "journeyed in the wilderness" to this New World Zion. Other iterations of this theme will include the newly converted Alma the Elder's flight from the court of King Noah and his founding of a church in the wilderness, and yet another people descended from Old World exiles, who cross the sea in barges after being commanded to "go forth into the wilderness" at the time of the Tower of Babel. Most poignantly of all, the record will close with the spectacle of a lonely Moroni, sole survivor of his race. Finding in his wilderness exile that he has neither family, friends, nor "whither to go," the successive chain of Zion-building finds its definitive end and the record closes thereafter.

The Book of Mormon may be seen in this light as the story of the unending transmission of the gospel into new contexts, a chronicle of the volatility and fragility of lands of refuge, a testament of the portability and ceaseless transmutations of Zion, with the only constant being the eternally present promise of a special relationship to God, and direct access to his power and truth. The original dislocation signified by Lehi's exodus becomes a prelude not to a new geographical gathering; rather, it points to the permanent reconstitution of Zion into spiritual refuge. The resonance of this theme for early American descendents of those who had embarked on their own errand into the wilderness would have been unmistakable. And the theme would undoubtedly have held special poignancy for the first readers of the Book of Mormon, nineteenth-century religious refugees who persisted doggedly and tragically in attempts to realize their own earthly Zions in a trail from Ohio through Missouri to Illinois and the Great Basin of Utah.

New configurations of scripture

In the 1830s, the Book of Mormon erupted out of an intensely Christian environment. Its most popular appellation, the Golden Bible, or the Mormon Bible, affirmed the fact that the Bible was its first and enduring standard of comparison and the point of departure for understanding it. Mormons called it scripture, the Word of God, a revelation. It was about Jews and the House of Israel, and its opening scenes are in Jerusalem, with language that is immediately recognizable as Tudor English. Early editions were even deliberately bound to emulate the most popular edition of the Bible in circulation in nineteenth-century America. Joseph Smith planned to publish an edition in which the two sacred volumes, the Bible and the Book of Mormon, would be bound together (a desire not realized until the twentieth century).

A striking difference between the Book of Mormon and the Bible is that the latter achieved its present form(s) through a long process that involved both identified and anonymous authors, almost entirely anonymous scribes and editors, Jewish and early Christian

4. First Editions of the Book of Mormon

councils, a good dose of faction and conflict, and centuries of transmission history marked by darkness and obscurity. The Book of Mormon, by contrast, is generally transparent about its own origins and construction from beginning to end. Clarity surrounding its provenance seems to be not just a by-product of such transparency, but central to its claim to authority and to what it has to say about the very nature of scripture and scriptural formation. Most writers are identified, and the entirety is organized and subsumed within the editorial control and prophetic vision of its final authors, Mormon and Moroni.

Its complex, multilayered, at times Chinese-box structure evinces important principles of how scripture is constituted. And the Book of Mormon itself is transparent about the process of its own metamorphosis from a panoply of sources and influences to the final product translated by Joseph Smith and delivered to the world as scripture. It will be useful therefore to trace the

35

organization and constitution of the text of the Book of Mormon from its beginnings.

After their eight-year sojourn in the Arabian wilderness and an oceanic crossing, Lehi's clan arrives in the promised land. Upon arrival, Nephi writes that the Lord commanded him to compile "the record of [his] people" (1 Ne. 19:1). He does not call it scripture or doctrine or prophecy—but a simple clan history. This account includes "the record of [his] father, and the genealogy of his fathers, and the more part of all [their] proceedings in the wilderness" (1 Ne. 19:2). And Nephi indicates that in the future, those plates are to contain "an account of the reign of the kings, and the wars and contentions of [his] people" (1 Ne. 9:4). They are, in other words, designed to be the record of what we today would call the political and secular history of his family and their descendents. Nephi obeys the command, fashioning "plates of ore" (they are never referred to in the Book of Mormon as gold plates) and commencing the record. He faithfully keeps that record for more than twenty years, at the end of which time he is directed by the Lord to fashion a second set of plates (subsequently called the "small plates" by Nephi's brother Jacob).

On these small plates, Nephi records "the ministry of [his] people" (1 Ne. 9:3). Elsewhere he describes the subject of the small plates as "the things of God" (1 Ne. 6:3), or "things . . . most precious" (Jac. 1.2). The pages constituting the first quarter of the modern Book of Mormon are entirely derived from these small plates. The command to produce two parallel records must have struck Nephi as peculiar, but he knows only that it is for "a wise purpose" of the Lord. For reasons we shall see in chapter 7 and that go a long way toward explaining the need for two histories, Smith's translation of Nephi's first version, written on the "other" or presumably large, plates and later abridged by Mormon, never made it into print. What this means for the reader is that for the first two hundred years and more of the history chronicled by the Book of Mormon, we have a focus on "ministry" rather than on history, written by Nephi and never subjected to later abridgment.

After explaining the origins of this record that will eventually become the Book of Mormon, and establishing his intent to write nothing "save it be...sacred," Nephi goes about constituting his record in a way that is markedly different from simple prophetic utterance or inspired dictate. He constitutes his record as a kind of bricolage, or assemblage of already existing pieces into a new mosaic. In doing so, he reinforces a conception of scripture as fluid, diffuse, and infinitely generable—the very opposite of scripture as unilinear, concretized, fixed in a canon.

The first eight chapters of his record Nephi characterizes as a summation of a record his father kept. His own record commences with the details leading up to his vision of the Tree of Life. He then assimilates into his account a number of other prophetic voices unknown to modern readers: "[Christ shall yield himself to] be lifted up, according to the words of Zenock, and to be crucified, according to the words of Neum, and to be buried in a sepulcher, according to the words of Zenos" (1 Ne. 19:10). (Nephi's brother Jacob will likewise borrow, but more extensively, from Zenos). Nephi then progresses to the prophecies of Isaiah, whose stature in Nephi's eyes is indicated by the fact that he refers to him simply as "the prophet." Not content to merely cite him, Nephi incorporates into his narrative entire swaths of Isaiah, largely unchanged from the form known to Jewish and Christian readers of the Bible. These writings of Isaiah, Nephi tells us, were contained in the brass plates that he took from Laban in Jerusalem. Those passages most favored by Nephi for inclusion are ones dealing with covenant, the scattering, and the gathering of Israel. As Nephi explains, "I did read unto them that which was written by the prophet Isaiah; for I did liken all scripture unto us, that it might be for our profit and learning" (1 Ne. 19:23). This aside reveals that Nephi is engaged in a kind of midrash on the Isaiah passages. Midrash is based on the word *derash*. As Norman Cohen explains,

> the derash teaches meaning for every age. The term derash is based
> on the root d-r-h, which means "to seek" or "to search out" in
> reference to the Bible, i.e., to search out and to discern meaning in
> the biblical text.... Derash, the method of midrash (from the same
> root), is, as we have seen already, the dominant mode for the
> creation of rabbinic literature.... [T]he words of the text can
> illumine the reader's life experience, while the reader, in bringing his
> or her life to bear on a text, can penetrate the human issues implicit
> in it. Derash essentially involves the "reading in" of a meaning
> different from the text's peshat [literal meaning].

Time and again, Nephi cites passages from Isaiah. When his brothers ask, "what meaneth these things which ye have read?," his explications situate his family and posterity firmly within the scope of Isaiah's vision of the future: "it meaneth us in the days to come, and also all our brethren who are of the house of Israel," he says in one typical interpretation (1 Ne. 22:1, 6).

The dynamic, vibrant life of scripture, as something that is generated, assimilated, transformed, and transmitted in endless ways and in ever new contexts, is clearly apparent in these scenes where Nephi centers in on his commission to produce a sacred record. This pattern achieves its most dramatic instance well into the subsequent narrative, with a repentant sinner, Alma the Elder. Coming from a heathen people far removed from the righteous Nephites, Alma begins, surprisingly, to preach Christ to his peers: "And now it came to pass that Alma, who had fled from the servants of King Noah, repented of his sins and iniquities, and ... began to teach ... concerning that which was to come, and also concerning the resurrection of the dead, and the redemption of the people, which was to be brought to pass through the power, and sufferings, and death of Christ." (Mos. 18:1–2).

How did Alma obtain knowledge of Christ? He heard the preaching of Abinadi, an itinerant prophet martyred by the wicked Noah. And Alma "did write all the words which Abinadi had spoken" (Mos. 17:4). Where did Abinadi, who appears suddenly in the narrative with no background or introduction, get his knowledge? In Mosiah 13–14 we find him reading the words of Moses and of Isaiah to Noah's court, and finding in them clear foreshadowing of a "God [who should] himself . . . come down among the children of men, and . . . redeem his people" (Mos.18:1). Where did Abinadi obtain those scriptures? He was a member of Zeniff's colony, which was an offshoot of the major Nephite settlement, and the narrative would apparently have us believe they took copies of the Nephite records with them when they departed Zarahemla and resettled Lehi-Nephi. And those Nephite records? As we already learned early in the Book of Mormon, Nephi and his brothers absconded with Laban's brass plates that contained the writings of Moses, Isaiah, and several other Hebrew prophets. So we have a clear line of transmission from prophetic utterance, to brass plates, to Nephi's small plates, to Zeniff's copy, to Abinadi's gloss, to Alma's transcription. And that is only half the story. From Alma, we learn that those teachings become a part of his written record. When he and his band of exiles arrive back in the major colony of Zarahemla, King Mosiah reads to the assembled people "the account of Alma and his brethren" (Mos. 25:6). King Mosiah, as guardian of the large plates, presumably incorporates the record into his own record. Those plates are subsequently abridged by Mormon, the late fourth-century Nephite editor.

It is in this conception of scripture that the boundary between Nephites and nineteenth-century Mormons, between Moroni and Joseph Smith, again fades. Not in the sense of the Book of Mormon as pseudepigrapha, but in the sense of its nineteenth-century incarnation as one more stage, one more version, of prophetic utterance that can never be permanently fixed or final.

As Nephi writes in a kind of celebration of this scriptural proliferation,

> I command all men, both in the east and in the west, and in the north, and in the south, and in the islands of the sea, that they shall write the words which I speak unto them.... For behold, I shall speak unto the Jews and they shall write it; and I shall also speak unto the Nephites and they shall write it; and I shall also speak unto the other tribes of the house of Israel, which I have led away, and they shall write it; and I shall also speak unto all nations of the earth and they shall write it. (2 Ne. 29:11-12)

After the mutiny on the HMS *Bounty* in 1789, the mutineers founded on Pitcairn Island a colony that rapidly descended into a nightmarish world of violence and debauchery. The settlement was on the verge of self-destruction. With the help of a Bible found among their effects, survivors founded a church and a school on the island. When the colony was discovered years later, the inhabitants were so orderly and educated that the criminals were not returned for trial.

The story may be somewhat romanticized, but its moral of the indispensability of scripture to cultural and spiritual preservation is echoed in the Book of Mormon. The civilization of the Nephites could be said to be founded on a blood sacrifice that attests the incalculable value of scripture. Nephi slew the corrupt Jewish leader Laban in order to secure the scriptural record engraved on the plates of brass. The manslaughter is expressly condoned, even mandated by the voice of the Spirit, which testifies to the reluctant Nephi that "it is better that one man should perish than that a nation should dwindle and perish in unbelief" (1 Ne. 4:13). The specter of a nation spiritually dying for lack of scripture subsequently becomes reality, when Nephi's descendents encounter another immigrant population in the New World, who departed Jerusalem at the time of Zedekiah's captivity, around 586 BCE. Of these "Mulekites," the chronicler Amaleki writes, "they had

40

become exceedingly numerous. Nevertheless, they had many wars and serious contentions, . . . their language had become corrupted; and they had brought no records with them; and they denied the being of their Creator; and Mosiah, nor the people of Mosiah, could understand them" (Omni 1:17).

Religious memory is clearly the only safeguard against spiritual apostasy and cultural decline. The injunction to remember becomes a mantra woven through the entire length of the Book of Mormon. Nephi and other prophets exhort their audience to "remember the words which I speak unto you," "remember to keep his commandments," "remember the Lord," "remember to observe the statutes and judgments of the Lord," "remember the greatness of the Holy One of Israel"—these and innumerable kindred commands are encapsulated in the oft-repeated injunction to remember "the covenants of the Father." The memory of the past is an essential guarantee that they will remember their obligation to the future, and thus maintain intact their covenant relationship with God. Memory preserves the links of this human chain against the ravages of sin and forgetting. So the injunction to remember "the captivity of their fathers," the "deliverance of our fathers," "the travails, and the labors, and the pains of the Jews," and in sum, "how merciful the Lord hath been unto the children of men, from the creation of Adam even down until the time that ye shall receive these things," is mirrored in the stimulus and prod to remember obligation extending into the future: "Remember your children," and "remember your seed." In this light, the indispensability of the scriptures is made resoundingly clear by Alma the Younger. In his simple explanation, "they have enlarged the memory of this people" (Alma 37:8).

Centrality of family

The first sentence of the Book of Mormon proper is the header, written by Nephi, in which he characterizes what is to follow as "an account of Lehi and his wife Sariah and his four sons." The Book of

Mormon, in other words, in fact and in the eyes of its first author, is the story of a family. In the text's introductory sentence, Nephi's first thought is to cast himself as a son of "goodly parents," "taught in all the learning of my father," tempered nonetheless by "many afflictions." The stage is immediately set for the kind of familiar domestic drama with which the patriarchal narratives of the Hebrew Bible abound. Like the righteous Abel, the favored Isaac, the usurper Jacob, and the indulged Joseph, Nephi is situated within a web of family relationships including righteous parents, scheming or displaced siblings, and a posterity's destiny hanging in the balance.

Of the many parallels with the Mosaic narratives invoked by Nephi, this comparison sets up the most emphatic reversal of all. For if the first brothers in Genesis are embroiled in fratricide, and bitter brotherly conflict persists through the generations including Ishmael, Esau, and Joseph's brothers, the epic history of the patriarchs finds happy resolution in the end. In the emotional ordeal Joseph imposes on his eleven guilty brothers in the realm of Pharaoh, followed by his frank forgiveness of them for selling him into bondage, we find atonement and family reconciliation. The emotionally cleansing scene of recognition and weeping, followed by reunion with Israel and establishment of the entire clan in Goshen, is capstoned by Jacob's patriarchal benediction upon the heads of his dozen children. Prophetic promises explicate and confirm the providentially guided destiny of the House of Israel. We end Genesis with closure, family unity, and intimations of great destinies.

Against this foil, the Book of Mormon's family saga acquires a somber cast. Sibling jealousies do not find resolution but violent expansion, culminating in a tragic and genocidal finale painfully deferred until the record's final pages. The founding family of the Book of Mormon fractures even before they leave Jerusalem. The eldest sons Laman and Lemuel murmur against their father's indictment of Jerusalem, their flight from the city, and his whole vision-led life that drags them into its disruptive wake. Murmuring escalates to contention, violence against the ever-obedient Nephi, and an eventual attempt on his life. After the harrowing ocean crossing and the death of clan leader Lehi, the group fractures permanently. On the pretext that Nephi has usurped their right to rule, a claim that will persist through centuries, Laman and Lemuel again plot violence against Nephi, who departs farther into the interior with his followers. His brother describes the principal dynamic that animates subsequent Book of Mormon history: the dissenters, left to possess the site of original settlement, conceive "an eternal hatred against us, their brethren. And they sought by the power of their arms to destroy us continually" (Jac. 7:24).

Because the record's first writer, Nephi, sees in vision the extinction of his people at the hands of their brethren, and the book's final writer and editor, Moroni, personally experiences the apocalypse, the narrative from beginning to end both anticipates and looks back upon a tragic history. To compound an already wretched tale, Moroni appends near the end an account of another civilization, the Jaredites, who centuries earlier met an equally calamitous end. Narratively, then, reunion and resolution are tentatively and fleetingly attained at best, and hope hovers perpetually over the horizon. The grounds for whatever solace there may be, the sole mode of consolation and vehicle of hope, is the sacred record itself. It will be the means, in a day far future, of recuperating a message of eternal worth that outlives the peoples who authored it. As the Lord reveals to a grieving Nephi, who has just witnessed in vision the cataclysms to fall upon his descendents:

> I will be merciful unto the Gentiles in that day, insomuch that I will bring forth unto them, in mine own power, much of my gospel, which shall be plain and precious, saith the Lamb. For, behold, saith the Lamb: I will manifest myself unto thy seed, that they shall write many things which I shall minister unto them, which shall be plain and precious; and after thy seed shall be destroyed, and

dwindle in unbelief, and also the seed of thy brethren, behold, these things shall be hid up, to come forth unto the Gentiles. (1 Ne. 13:34–35)

But the tragedy is not as complete as those words suggest, for Nephi also receives the assurance that at least a remnant of his posterity will survive both the ravages of the civil wars and the later depredations of the "Gentile" colonizers (1 Ne. 13:30).

The qualification is crucial, because it grounds the fragile hope that motivates and animates the maintenance of the sacred records for a thousand years and more. This is no chronicle kept by court historians or apocalyptic warning legalistically recorded by a dour Jeremiah or a Jonah waiting with Schadenfreude for the violent denouement. It is first and foremost a father's testament and family history, impelled by parental anxiety. It is written to inspire, to edify, to morally instruct, and to warn an extended family already riven by dissension and faithlessness.

When Lehi is first introduced to us, he has the unenviable task of trying to forefend the destruction of Jerusalem and its people. Though he wrestles with national destinies, the fate of his own family is his overriding concern, and the local domestic tragedy he fails to avert becomes in this regard a microcosm, or a type, of the larger tragedy it portends. Lehi's vision of the Tree of Life, as we learn from two retellings of it, expands to involve contemporary events in Jerusalem, the destiny of scattered Israel, and the coming of Messiah. But Lehi, in his first retelling of the story, seems unable to move beyond the personal source of grief the vision elicited. The same seems true of Nephi, who records, "These are the words of my father: ... And Laman and Lemuel partook not of the fruit, said my father." And even though Lehi at this time discusses other matters pertaining to his vision ("all the words of his dream ... were many"), Nephi only notes that "because of these things which he saw in vision, he exceedingly feared for Laman and Lemuel, yea he feared lest they should be cast off from the presence of the Lord. And he did exhort them then with all the feeling of a tender parent, that they would hearken to his words" (1 Ne. 8:34–37).

Like the Old Testament, then, family stories dominate the subject matter of the early sections of the Book of Mormon. But they also pervade and eventually conclude the narrative as well. The poignant concern of Lehi for his sons is mirrored later in the paternal worry of King Mosiah for his missionary sons about to proselytize a violent and hostile people in Lamanite territory. His fears are allayed when he obtains a revelation expressly telling him, "Let them go up, for many shall believe on their words, and they shall have eternal life; and I will deliver thy sons out of the hands of the Lamanites" (Mos. 28:7). The righteous Alma the Elder has a particularly recalcitrant son, who goes about seeking to destroy the Church his father founded. When an angel appears to Alma the Younger in an episode reminiscent of Paul on the road to Damascus, the miraculous conversion that ensues is traceable to a father's love. "The Lord hath heard the prayers of his people," the angel tells the stunned youth, "and also the prayers of his servant, Alma, who is thy father; for he has prayed with much faith concerning thee that thou mightest be brought to the knowledge of the truth; therefore, for this purpose have I come to convince thee of the power and authority of God, that the prayers of his servants might be answered according to their faith" (Mos. 27:14).

Even without angelic intervention, the power of loving parents proves potent. Nephi implicitly attributes all that is good in his life to "his goodly parents," and having been taught "in all the learning of my father" (1 Ne. 1:1). The first conversion recorded in the Book of Mormon occurs when Enos goes to the forest to hunt, and, as he writes, "the words which I had often heard my father speak concerning eternal life, and the joy of the saints, sunk deep into my heart" (Enos 1:4). The miraculous preservation of the warrior youths of Helaman, which we will see in chapter 3, is expressly attributed by them to their having "been taught by their

45

mothers, that if they did not doubt, God would deliver them" (Alma 56:47). And the last two characters given voice in the Book of Mormon, silhouetted against a battlefield of appalling carnage, are the warrior prophets Mormon and his son Moroni, who vainly battled to save their people, by preaching and by force of arms, from a spiral into irredeemable depravity and death.

When the final scene wraps up, as when the thousand-year drama began, fragile hope resides in the son who occupies a darkening stage. The family tragedy that escalated into a civilization's utter destruction is reduced in the end, once again, to loss that is profoundly personal and relational. The abstractions of historic catastrophe collapse into a family circle. The seeds of destruction, the hope of spiritual survival, and the consequences of evil never really move outside the local and the personal.

With his last words, Mormon laments the scene before him:

> My soul was rent with anguish, because of the slain of my people, and I cried: O ye fair ones, how could ye have departed from the ways of the Lord! O ye fair ones, how could ye have rejected that Jesus, who stood with open arms to receive you! Behold, if ye had not done this, ye would not have fallen. But behold, ye are fallen, and I mourn your loss. O ye fair sons and daughters, ye fathers and mothers, ye husbands and wives, ye fair ones, how is it that ye could have fallen! (Morm. 6:16–19)

When Moroni appends an epilogue to Mormon's final narrative, pain receives its full complement in his isolation from all human relationships.

> And my father also was killed by them, and I even remain alone to write the sad tale of the destruction of my people. . . . My father hath been slain in battle, and all my kinsfolk, and I have not friends nor whither to go; and how long the Lord will suffer that I may live, I know not. (Morm. 8:3, 5)

46

Chapter 3
Stories and characters

Recent years have witnessed growing attention to the power of story to convey theological meaning. Narrative theology has arisen largely because it provides a way to value a biblical text that has lost its power to command respect on the basis of its claims to historical validity or propositional revelation. The Book of Mormon is emphatic, as we have seen, in reaffirming both. There is little motivation, therefore, to find in Book of Mormon narratives theological meanings that accrue from narrative structure or literary tropes. That is not to say the material for such analysis is not ready to hand. We have seen the prevalence of a number of themes that incorporate familiar elements of biblical Christianity into new patterns of meaning. Those themes run through the Book of Mormon from beginning to end, and constitute fairly explicit preoccupations of Nephi, Mormon, and other principal writers. Like the Bible with its stories of Samson, Jonah, or Lazarus, the Book of Mormon also contains numerous self-contained episodes of intrinsic beauty and interest. A sampling of these stories not only suggests the range of characters and plots that fill the pages of this scripture, but extends the range of values informing the Book of Mormon narrative. Some of these stories powerfully teach particular principles, like the sanctity of covenant making or the interdependence of political and spiritual liberty. Others are disturbingly realistic, depicting the tragic consequences of spiritual degradation, or plumbing with psychological realism the stupefaction that results from moral apathy.

Helaman's stripling warriors

One of the more striking juxtapositions in the Book of Mormon are twinned stories of steadfast pacifism and lethally efficient militarism—unfolding in the same tribe in contiguous moments. Often read in Mormon culture as prolonged proof texts about pacifism or "just" wars respectively, it is out of the tension arising from the two that a distinct moral emerges that trumps both. The episodes begin with the most famous conversion story in the Book of Mormon—that of Alma the Younger and his four companions in spiritual delinquency, the sons of the Nephite king Mosiah. All become the most intrepid, successful missionaries described in the Book of Mormon. Going into the heart of the Lamanite territory, ruled over by inveterate enemies of the Nephites, Mosiah's son Ammon achieves especially miraculous results. Imprisoned upon entering King Lamoni's domain, he asks to be made a servant. He saves the king's flocks from bandits, wins his trust, and converts him to belief in God. The work of conversion spreads to the supreme ruler over the Lamanites, but incites resentment and rebellion among the unconverted, who prepare for war against the intruder faith. The leader of the newly converted, who rename themselves "Anti-Nephi-Lehies," now makes a remarkable decision:

> And now, my brethren, if our brethren seek to destroy us, behold, we will hide away our swords, yea, even we will bury them deep in the earth, that they may be kept bright, as a testimony that we have never used them, at the last day; and if our brethren destroy us, behold, we shall go to our God and shall be saved. And now it came to pass that when the king had made an end of these sayings, and all the people were assembled together, they took their swords, and all the weapons which were used for the shedding of blood, and they did bury them up deep in the earth. (Alma 24:16–17)

Their enemies are not impressed. They fall upon the defenseless pacifists, slaughtering them by the hundreds. Some of the more humane Lamanites sicken of the one-sided carnage, and with hearts "swollen in them for those of their brethren who had fallen under the sword, ... threw down their weapons of war, and they would not take them again, for they were stung for the murders which they had committed; and they came down even as their brethren, relying upon the mercies of those whose arms were lifted to slay them" (Alma 24:24–25). But the merciful are the minority, and soon Ammon and his converts realize they must be compliant in their own genocide or flee to safety.

The Nephites agree to give them sanctuary in the land of Jershon, and so stay their destruction. Over the ensuing generation, the Anti-Nephi-Lehies dwell safely in Jershon, while civil war engulfs the region. Overwhelmed with guilt, and regretting an oath that makes them passive witnesses to the destruction of their protectors, they determine to break their vow and assist the Nephites. Helaman, son of Alma the Younger, has inherited his father's office, and vigorously dissuades them from doing so. It is at this juncture that a novel solution is proposed:

> But behold, ... they had many sons, who had not entered into a covenant that they would not take their weapons of war to defend themselves against their enemies; therefore they did assemble themselves together at this time, as many as were able to take up arms, ... and they entered into a covenant to fight for the liberty of the Nephites, yea, to protect the land unto the laying down of their lives ... and they would that Helaman should be their leader. (Alma 53:16–19)

As an army these two thousand "stripling soldiers" are young and untried, but they are exemplary in their faithfulness. "They were exceedingly valiant for courage, and also for strength and activity; but behold, this was not all—they were men who were true at all times in whatsoever thing they were entrusted. Yea, they were men of truth and soberness, for they had been taught to keep the commandments of God and to walk uprightly before him" (Alma 53:20–21).

Part of their righteousness is rooted in the reluctance with which they take up arms. As Helaman prepares them for combat, he asks, "What say ye, my sons, will ye go against them to battle?" and they reply, "Father, behold our God is with us, and he will not suffer that we should fall; then let us go forth; we would not slay our brethren if they would let us alone" (Alma 56:46).

What ensues is one of the great miracles of the Book of Mormon:

> But behold, my little band of two thousand and sixty fought most desperately; yea, they were firm before the Lamanites, and did administer death unto all those who opposed them. And as the remainder of our army were about to give way before the Lamanites, behold, those two thousand and sixty were firm and undaunted. Yea, and they did obey and observe to perform every word of command with exactness.... And it came to pass that after the Lamanites had fled, I immediately gave orders that my men who had been wounded should be taken from among the dead, and caused that their wounds should be dressed. And it came to pass that there were two hundred, out of my two thousand and sixty, who had fainted because of the loss of blood; nevertheless, according to the goodness of God, and to our great astonishment, and also the joy of our whole army, there was not one soul of them who did perish; yea, and neither was there one soul among them who had not received many wounds.... Now this was the faith of these of whom I have spoken; they are young, and their minds are firm, and they do put their trust in God continually. (Alma 57:19–27)

The power of this story derives from what first appears to be its moral ambiguity. Two groups, separated only by a generation, are lauded respectively for their pacifism even at the cost of life, and for their valor and disciplined effectiveness as warriors. Yet the former are not condemned for inaction in the face of national peril and the death of their protectors. And their children are not condemned for their armed struggle against their former brethren. In a thousand-year epic drenched in blood and peopled by warrior-prophets, righteous violence would seem to have the implicit privilege. The moral of this story, where righteous pacifism and righteous warfare find comfortable co-existence, would seem to be that faithfulness to covenants righteously entered into trumps both. The Anti-Nephi-Lehies "had entered into a covenant and they would not break it" (Alma 43:11). By the identical token, their sons "entered into a covenant to fight for the liberty of the Nephites" (Alma 53:17). In the Book of Mormon, covenant is the thread of safety on which the survival, spiritual safety, and very identity of the people hang. Nephi had invoked God's covenant with Israel in the very first verses of Isaiah that he reads to his family, marooned and isolated in a wilderness a seeming eternity away from the Promised Land they had known. "Hear ye the words of the prophet," he had consoled them, "ye who are a remnant of the House of Israel, a branch who have been broken off; . . . liken them unto yourselves, that ye may have hope as well as your brethren . . . (1 Ne. 19:24). Subsequently, covenants guarantee to Nephi the survival of his race, to Enos the salvation of his soul, and to their people, the coming of a Messiah.

Captain Moroni

In the century before Christ, the internecine warfare between Nephites and Lamanites intensifies. While Alma the Younger and the sons of Mosiah employ the word of God to bring peace, Moroni employs the sword. He is to righteous militancy what Alma is to missionary fervor. Not to be confused with the last author of the Book of Mormon, who seals the record and witnesses the destruction of his people, this Moroni is chief captain of the Nephite armies in the year 74 BCE. Moroni's watchword is liberty, and when he leads his people in combat, he "inspire[s] their hearts with these thoughts—yea, the thoughts of their lands, their liberty, yea, their freedom from bondage" (Alma 43:48). The situation in the Nephite homeland goes from merely bad to "exceedingly precarious and dangerous" when political dissidents take advantage of external crisis to foment division and subversion of freedom within the government. The ambitious Amalickiah conspires "to destroy the foundation of liberty" among the Nephites and install himself as king. Moroni's response is both vehement and uncompromising:

> he rent his coat; and he took a piece thereof, and wrote upon it—In memory of our God, our religion, and freedom, and our peace, our wives, and our children—and he fastened it upon the end of a pole ... (and he called it the title of liberty).

Then after girding himself with armor, and praying for God's blessings,

> he went forth among the people, waving the rent part of his garment in the air, that all might see the writing which he had written upon the rent part, and crying with a loud voice, saying: Behold, whosoever will maintain this title upon the land, let them come forth in the strength of the Lord, and enter into a covenant that they will maintain their rights, and their religion, that the Lord God may bless them. And it came to pass that when Moroni had proclaimed these words, behold, the people came running together with their armor girded about their loins, rending their garments in token, or as a covenant. (Alma 46:19–21)

With his strengthened armies, Moroni defeats the armies of Amalickiah, their leader flees, and the defeated dissenters are captured. As a condition of clemency, Moroni requires them to "enter into a covenant to support the cause of freedom." Those who refuse to so covenant are put to death.

Moroni's zeal in promoting and defending liberty, and his intolerance for neutrality and inaction, culminate in a near-tragic

misunderstanding that calls forth one of the greatest
manifestations of human generosity in the whole bloody saga of
fratricidal war. As he is on the point of turning the tide against
the aggressor Lamanites, military support to the armies of his
subordinate Helaman abruptly ceases, and the momentum is lost.
In his frustration, Moroni writes a blistering letter to Pahoran,
head of the Nephite government. "We desire to know the cause of
your thoughtless state," he writes.

> Can you think to sit upon your thrones in a state of thoughtless
> stupor, while your enemies are spreading the work of death around
> you? Yea, while they are murdering thousands of your
> brethren . . . who have looked up to you for protection. . . . But why
> should I say much concerning this matter? For we know not but
> what ye yourselves are seeking for authority. We know not but what
> ye are also traitors to your country. (Alma 60:6–8, 18)

And then the dire threat:

> Except ye do repent of that which ye have done, and begin to be up
> and doing, and send forth food and men unto us, . . . I will come unto
> you, and if there be any among you that has a desire for freedom, yea,
> if there be even a spark of freedom remaining, behold I will stir up
> insurrections among you, even until those who have desires to usurp
> power and authority shall become extinct. Yea, behold, I do not fear
> your power nor your authority. . . . Behold, I am Moroni, your chief
> captain. I seek not for power, but to pull it down. I seek not for honor
> of the world, but for the glory of my God, and the freedom and
> welfare of my country. An thus I close my epistle. (Alma 60:24–36)

The real state of affairs, we learn, is quite different from what
Moroni had inferred. Traitors had arisen in the homeland, allied
themselves with the Lamanites, and driven the government into
exile. Pahoran had been more hard pressed in his own campaign
than the armies on the frontier. And then, in his response,
we see Pahoran's magnanimity overshadow even Moroni's

righteous outrage: "And now, in your epistle you have censured me, but it mattereth not; I am not angry, but do rejoice in the greatness of your heart." And then invoking Moroni's military assistance, he closes his epistle to his "beloved brother, Moroni" (Alma 61:9, 21).

Moroni's uncompromising intolerance for slackness, his violent repression of dissent and his impetuous judgment, make him a stark counterpoint to his contemporaries, the long-suffering Alma and the pacifist converts of Ammon. But he seems to be the preferred hero of the book's editor Mormon, himself a general caught up on the losing side of an apocalyptic war. "Verily I say unto you," he writes, "if all men had been, and were, and ever would be, like unto Moroni, behold, the very powers of hell would have been shaken forever; yea, the devil would never have power over the hearts of men" (Alma 48:17).

Martyrdom in Ammonihah

Not all Book of Mormon stories are uplifting or even faith-affirming. This scripture can also present us with scenes of carnage and brutality, apocalypse, and unmitigated suffering. One such story is the tale of a missionary journey with unexpectedly disastrous consequences.

Almost five centuries after settlement, the tribal religion of the Israelite settlers had become contaminated by widespread secularism and unbelief. Consequently, Alma the Elder organized several branches of a proto-Christian church. His son, Alma the Younger, who had spent much his youth subverting his father's ministry becomes, after his Paul-like conversion, a powerful political, military, and religious leader. At this time in Nephite history, reversing the Old Testament pattern, the monarchy of the Nephites is transformed into a rule of judges, and Alma is appointed first chief judge and governor, as well as high priest. Alarmed by the spiritual degeneracy of his people, Alma relinquishes his political office and embarks on a missionary journey of revival and renewal. His sermons on Christ's atonement, faith, humility, and obedience are a principal source of recorded doctrinal teachings in the Book of Mormon.

He wins thousands of converts and is phenomenally successfully in bringing entire cities to repentance—and then he visits the people of Ammonihah. Impervious to his crusade, the hard-hearted citizens revile him, spit upon him, and cast him out. Leaving the city in defeat, he is visited by an angel, who commands him to return and persist in his message of warning. He does so, encounters a righteous citizen named Amulek, and together they turn to the task of preaching to a resistant populace. They expound powerful sermons, prophecy of Christ, and rebuke an anti-Christ. They are thrown into prison for their efforts. With Alma's record of success, divine mandate, angelic assurance, and powerful missionary companion, the stage is set for miraculous deliverance. But when Alma and Amulek are released, it is not at the hand of an angel. Rather, they are escorted by their captors to a scene of appalling horror. The male population who believed their words have been exiled from the city. Its leaders now

> brought their wives and children together, and whosoever believed or had been taught to believe in the word of God they caused that they should be cast into the fire. . . . And it came to pass that they took Alma and Amulek, and carried them forth to the place of martyrdom, that they might witness the destruction of those who were consumed by fire. And when Amulek saw the pains of the women and children who were consuming in the fire, he also was pained. (Alma 14:8–10)

Deliverance comes at last to the missionary pair—but it does little to compensate for the harrowing cost of their dogged persistence in following divine commands. True enough, the martyred women and children are received by the Lord in glory, we are told (Alma

14:11), while the people of Ammonihah will eventually be obliterated by Lamanite armies (Alma 16:2–3). But we do not see either scenario—only the immolation of the innocent, including, horrifyingly, Amulek's own family (See Alma 10:11; 15:18). Mormon's emphasis is firmly on the tragic realism of the here and now, in which a costly salvation is worked out.

Gadianton Robbers

Two principal forms of retribution afflict the Nephites as they fall into the recurrent cycle of blessed prosperity followed by sinful pride. The first are the Lamanites themselves who, as the Lord warned, are "a scourge unto [the Nephite] seed, to stir them up in the ways of remembrance" (1 Ne. 2:24). When this internecine war is not decimating the population, it is repeatedly vexed by corruption within that takes the form of sophisticated conspiratorial enterprises known as "secret combinations." The dominant manifestation of this scourge becomes known as the Gadianton Robbers. This ancient mafia erupts on the scene in the time of Helaman's son Nephi, a few decades before Christ. The many layered story Mormon relates is striking not for its depiction of physical violence and destruction, seen so often in Book of Mormon warfare. This is rather a portrait of the psychological dimensions of evil, and takes us from hypocrisy and self-justification through willful blindness and stupidity to what may be the most chilling stage of all—blithe indifference to one's own complicity in the moral decay of a society.

At this time, the Nephites have fallen to such depths of depravity that in a striking reversal, the Lamanites send missionaries to exhort them to repentance. Wickedness grows into intrigue and political subversion; the chief judge is murdered "as he sat upon the judgment seat" by one Kishkumen, chieftain of a band of outlaws. His son and successor is likewise murdered shortly thereafter by followers of Kishkumen's successor, Gadianton, who in turn usurp control of the government.

Like Alma before him, the righteous chief judge Nephi resigns his position to devote himself to preaching. Returning from a fruitless missionary journey, and consumed by his grief over the enveloping wickedness, Nephi pours out his heart in eloquent sorrow upon his garden tower: "Oh, that I could have had my days in the days when my father Nephi first came out of the land of Jerusalem, that I could have joyed with him in the promised land; then were his people easy to be entreated" (Hel. 7:7). His lament was impassioned and public enough that when he arose, a crowd had assembled. Observing the crowd, who are merely curious rather than shamed by his litany of their evils, Nephi turns from lament to sharp rebuke, indicting the people for their corruption and predicting dire consequences if they do not repent. As the offended rabble call for his arrest, others defend him, and the discord escalates into a near riot. At the height of the contention, an exasperated Nephi reveals to them a greater evil even then unfolding. At this very moment, he challenges the throng, "go ye in unto the judgment-seat, and search; and behold, your judge is murdered, and he lieth in his blood" (Hel. 8:27). The crowd apparently reacts with disbelief or indifference, except for five who race to the judgment-seat to verify his words. Arriving there, they witness the scene he described, and the shock overwhelms them.

They are arrested for the crime, and are released only when judges who were present at the scene in Nephi's garden explain what has happened. At this stage of the tragedy, and almost unbelievably, those same judges now demand the arrest of Nephi for the crime. And so a people made obtuse by their intransigent self-justification, confound prophesy with complicity and arraign the man of God. So in a last bid for moral clarity (and self-exoneration), Nephi demands that his accusers confront the murdered judge's brother. He predicts the precise words that man, the true murderer, shall speak by way of response, and where they shall find the incriminating blood of the victim. Once again they rush to verify his words—but this time the guilty party incriminates himself exactly as predicted, and there is nothing left to do but set Nephi at liberty.

It is in the aftermath of this tale that its subtle but unmistakable poignancy comes out:

> And now there were some among the people, who said that Nephi was a prophet. And there were others who said: Behold, he is a god, for except he was a god he could not know of all things.... And it came to pass that there arose a division among the people, insomuch that they divided hither and thither and went their ways, leaving Nephi alone, as he was standing in the midst of them. (Hel. 9:40–10:1)

No self-reproach or public indignation. No sorrow unto repentance. Just an irrepressible talent for turning resolution into discord, and revelation into debate. And the final response of a people who have themselves countenanced murder in high places, constituted themselves a lynch mob intent upon destroying the innocent, and had their corruption and hypocrisy exposed to the full light of day? Bemused wonder that resolves itself into the most complete indifference. It is a pathetic portrait of a people too desensitized to be shocked by their own—or anyone else's—depravity. Their self-indictment, like the bloody garments of a fratricide, merits barely a shrug. The final scene of a stunned and solitary Nephi figures the loneliness of the righteous few who remain in this spiritual wasteland.

These and other narratives in the Book of Mormon offer a rich array of stories that further the record's principal objectives, testifying to God's active participation in human lives and national destinies, affirming the rewards of righteousness, and the dangers of moral lassitude and complacency. They also have come to constitute a cultural grammar unique to Latter-day Saints. Mormon children sing a stirring anthem likening themselves to "the armies of Helaman," and commemorate in another song

Nephi's faithfulness in retrieving the brass plates from Laban. Mormons especially orthodox in their observance are called "iron rod" Mormons, after the symbol from Nephi's dream. (Those more inclined to interpretive freedom in their observance are "Liahona" Mormons.) Parents of wayward children console themselves with the precedent of the righteous but disappointed parents Lehi and Sariah. Missionaries aspire to emulate the phenomenally successful sons of Mosiah, or the intrepid "Samuel the Lamanite," who preached from a city wall, undeterred and untouched by a torrent of missiles launched against him by an unappreciative city. Like the tales of Samson or David and Goliath, such stories have acquired in Mormon culture an existence and a meaning independent of the context in which they first appeared.

Chapter 4
The Book of Mormon as literature

Goethe called the book of Ruth the greatest short story in world literature. The Psalms are poems of such masterful composition that they have inspired multitudes of poets to imitate them and recast them, in efforts to ever more perfectly capture their exemplary lyricism. Great scholars like Erich Auerbach find in Genesis a mode of narrative exposition that sustains comparison with the best of Homer, and the most resonant creations of Milton and Blake are but pale shadows of their biblical sources.

Measured against such a standard, the Book of Mormon finds few champions. Still, it took Christianity centuries to develop an artistic tradition that was inspired and shaped by recognition of the Bible's aesthetic value. Latter-day Saints are still learning to imbibe the Book of Mormon's doctrinal significance and make it a part of their cultural grammar. In some ways, the comparison is unfair, or at least inapt. The Bible is of course a compendium of genres, including wisdom literature, poetry, and psalms, in addition to extensive prophetic excurses. The Book of Mormon, however, is principally a clan history, the latter sections especially emphasizing political and military events. Nephi himself describes the large plates, constituting the bulk of the record, as consisting of "the reign of the kings and the wars and contentions of my people" (1 Ne. 9:4). Searching for literary wonders in the Book of Mormon is a bit like seeking lyrical inspiration in the books of Chronicles or Judges.

The Book of Mormon is a work of substantial complexity, however, with numerous well-spun narratives subsumed within a larger, comprehensive vision. There is a neat symmetry to the Bible as we have received it. Primordial creation is balanced by apocalypse and heavenly postscript. Time and its human drama are bookended by two eternities. The Tree of Knowledge that precipitates the human catastrophe in the opening pages, with its then-banned companion Tree of Life, is mirrored by that same Tree of Life encountered again in the heavenly realms, where man is invited, rather than forbidden, to partake. The resolution makes for comedy in Dante's sense of the word. All tears are wiped away, and the primal fall and alienation are remedied by reunion under the beneficent reign of God the Father.

The Book of Mormon is a tighter narrative, with a view that is constructed by editorial choices and intervention, rather than by the unfolding of cosmic history. And that view is a decidedly tragic one. To approach the Book of Mormon as literature is first and foremost to recognize it as the creation of a narrative voice, Mormon, who abridges and edits a thousand years of history in accordance with his perspective situated just this side of an Armageddon that he witnesses and in which he anticipates he will perish. The "land of promise" so touted in the epic's opening sections has now become a term of bitter irony. Mormon uses the expression five times, twice referring to the Old World, and the other three times looking back to the glory days of first settlement. "Oh, that I could have had my days in the days when my father Nephi first came out of the land of Jerusalem, that I could have joyed with him in the promised land," reminiscences one character (Nephi, son of Helaman, in Hel. 7: 7). As his people rush headlong to their destruction, the narrator's methodical invocation of each passing year tolls like a grim countdown to annihilation: "In the seventy and second year of the reign of the judges . . . the contentions did increase"; "And thus in the commencement of this, the thirtieth year, they were in a state of awful wickedness"; "And now it came to pass in the two hundred and thirty and first year, there was a great division among the people"; "And it came to pass in the three hundred and forty and sixth year [the Lamanites] began to come upon us again" (Hel. 11:1; 3 Ne. 6:17; 4 Ne. 1:36; Morm. 2:22).

The narrative has both epic sweep and heroic failure. The mighty general Mormon's expression of hopelessness is stark in its despairing simplicity. "Behold, I had led them, notwithstanding their wickedness I had led them many times to battle, and had loved them, according to the love of God which was in me, with all my heart; and my soul had been poured out in prayer unto my God all the day long for them; nevertheless, it was without faith, because of the hardness of their hearts" (Moro. 3:12).

The Bible's literary elegance makes it is a rich resource for liturgical purposes. The Mormons have no recitations or readings in their worship service, but there are enough moments of lyrical beauty in the Book of Mormon to meet such a purpose were they needed. Nephi, for example, can digress from his narrative occasionally to interpose his own poetic compositions, the most famous of which Mormons refer to as the psalm of Nephi.

Helaman's exhortation to ground oneself in Christ is too prosaic for a psalm, but it is rich in imagery and praise alike:

> And now, my sons, remember, remember that it is upon the rock of our Redeemer, who is Christ, the Son of God, that ye must build your foundation; that when the devil shall send forth his mighty winds, yea, his shafts in the whirlwind, yea, when all his hail and his mighty storm shall beat upon you, it shall have no power over you to drag you down to the gulf of misery and endless wo, because of the rock upon which ye are built, which is a sure foundation, a foundation whereon if men build they cannot fall. (Hel. 5:12)

Box 4.1

Nephi's psalm

Behold, my soul delighteth in the things of the Lord; and my heart pondereth continually upon the things which I have seen and heard.

Nevertheless, notwithstanding the great goodness of the Lord, in showing me his great and marvelous works, my heart exclaimeth: O wretched man that I am! Yea, my heart sorroweth because of my flesh; my soul grieveth because of mine iniquities.

I am encompassed about, because of the temptations and the sins which do so easily beset me.

And when I desire to rejoice, my heart groaneth because of my sins; nevertheless, I know in whom I have trusted.

My God hath been my support; he hath led me through mine afflictions in the wilderness; and he hath preserved me upon the waters of the great deep.

He hath filled me with his love, even unto the consuming of my flesh.

He hath confounded mine enemies, unto the causing of them to quake before me.

Behold, he hath heard my cry by day, and he hath given me knowledge by visions in the nighttime.

And by day have I waxed bold in mighty prayer before him; yea, my voice have I sent up on high; and angels came down and ministered unto me.

And upon the wings of his Spirit hath my body been carried away upon exceedingly high mountains. And mine eyes have beheld great things, yea, even too great for man; therefore I was bidden that I should not write them.

(*continued*)

Box 4.1 (Continued)

O then, if I have seen so great things, if the Lord in his condescension unto the children of men hath visited men in so much mercy, why should my heart weep and my soul linger in the valley of sorrow, and my flesh waste away, and my strength slacken, because of mine afflictions?

And why should I yield to sin, because of my flesh? Yea, why should I give way to temptations, that the evil one have place in my heart to destroy my peace and afflict my soul? Why am I angry because of mine enemy?

Awake, my soul! No longer droop in sin. Rejoice, O my heart, and give place no more for the enemy of my soul.

Do not anger again because of mine enemies. Do not slacken my strength because of mine afflictions.

Rejoice, O my heart, and cry unto the Lord, and say: O Lord, I will praise thee forever; yea, my soul will rejoice in thee, my God, and the rock of my salvation...

Yea, I know that God will give liberally to him that asketh. Yea, my God will give me, if I ask not amiss; therefore I will lift up my voice unto thee; yea, I will cry unto thee, my God, the rock of my righteousness. Behold, my voice shall forever ascend up unto thee, my rock and mine everlasting God. Amen. (2 Nephi 4:17–35)

Elsewhere we find repetition and parallelism used to poetic effect, as in Nephi's simple,

I glory in plainness;
I glory in truth:
I glory in my Jesus,
for he hath redeemed my soul from hell. (2 Ne. 33:6)

and Alma's exhortation to his son:

> O, remember, my son, and learn wisdom in thy youth; yea, learn in
> thy youth to keep the commandments of God.
> Yea, and cry unto God for all thy support; yea, let all thy doings be
> unto the Lord, and whithersoever thou goest let it be in the Lord;
> yea, let all thy thoughts be directed unto the Lord; yea, let the
> affections of thy heart be placed upon the Lord forever.
> Counsel with the Lord in all thy doings, and he will direct
> thee for good; yea, when thou liest down at night lie down unto
> the Lord, that he may watch over you in your sleep; and when
> thou risest in the morning let thy heart be full of thanks unto
> God; and if ye do these things, ye shall be lifted up at the last
> day. (Alma 37:36-37)

There are also more complex poetic conventions such as a version
of reverse parallelism called chiasmus (named for the Greek letter
X, which alludes to the convex structure of the poem). King
Benjamin, for example, declares the terms of a covenant in a form
that clearly reflects this configuration:

(a) And now... whosoever shall not take upon them the name of
Christ

  (b) must be called by some other name;

    (c) therefore, he findeth himself on the left hand of God.

      (d) And I would that ye should remember also, that this is
the name...

        (e) that never should be blotted out,

          (f) except it be through transgression; therefore,

          (f') take heed that ye do not transgress,

        (e') that the name be not blotted out of your hearts....

      (d') I would that ye should remember to retain the name...

    (c') that ye are not found on the left hand of God,

  (b') but that ye hear and know the voice by which ye shall be
called,

(a') and also, the name by which he shall call you. (Mos. 5:10-12)

Alma recounts his conversion narrative in an even more elaborately wrought chiasmus that occupies a full thirty verses. Form echoes content, when the composition climaxes and then reverses direction at the moment when he recognizes Christ's saving power:

Box 4.2

Alma's conversion: A chiasmus

(e) ...For I went about with the sons of Mosiah, seeking to *destroy the church of God;* but behold, God sent his holy angel to stop us by the way....

    (f) And it came to pass that *I fell to the earth;* and it was for the space of three days and three nights that I could not open my mouth,

        (g) *neither had I the use of my limbs* ...

            (h) Oh, thought I, that I could be banished and become extinct both soul and body, *that I might not be brought to stand in the presence of my God,* to be judged of my deeds.

                (i) And now, for three days and for three nights was I *racked, even with the pains of a damned soul.*

                    (j) And it came to pass that as I was thus racked with torment, ... I remembered also to have heard my father prophesy unto the people concerning the coming of one *Jesus Christ, a Son of God,*

(k) to *atone* for the sins
of the world.

(j') Now, as my mind caught
hold upon this thought,
I cried within my heart:
O *Jesus, thou Son of God*, have
mercy on me, who am in
the gall of bitterness, and
am encircled about by the
everlasting chains of
death.

(i') And now, behold, when I
thought this, I could remember
my pains no more; yea, I was
*harrowed up by the memory of my sins
no more* . . .

(h') Yea, methought I saw, even as our
father Lehi saw, God sitting upon his throne,
surrounded with numberless concourses
of angels, in the attitude of singing and
praising their God; yea, and *my soul did long
to be there.*

(g') But behold, *my limbs did receive their strength again*,
and

(f') *I stood upon my feet*, and did manifest unto the people
that I had been born of God.

(e') Yea, and from that time even until now, I have labored
without ceasing, that I might *bring souls unto repentance*; that I
might bring them to taste of the exceeding joy of which I did
taste; that they might also be born of God, and be filled with the
Holy Ghost. (Alma 36:6–24)

Mark Twain may have found the Book of Mormon to be "chloroform in print," and its King James idiom, much reliance on Isaiah, and deadening formulaic repetitions (1,300-plus verses begin with a form of "And it came to pass,") can make for heavy going. But these are more than compensated for by moments of conspicuous poetry, pathos, and literary complexity.

Chapter 5
Teachings

Gospel of faith, repentance, baptism, Holy Ghost

Surprising to many first-time readers of the Book of Mormon is just how unsurprising most of its doctrinal content is. First-generation convert John Murdock was certain that if the Mormon missionaries were true emissaries of God, "the Book of Mormon will contain the same plan of salvation as the Bible." He read the Book of Mormon, and "the spirit of the Lord rested on me, witnessing to me of the truth of the work." And Orson Pratt said that when he heard the message of Mormonism, "As soon as the sound penetrated my ears, I knew that if the Bible was true, their doctrine was true." Eli Gilbert, another early convert, wrote that when presented with a Book of Mormon, he "compared it with ... the bible, (which book I verily thought I believed,) and found the two books mutually and reciprocally corroborate each other; and if I let go the book of Mormon, the bible might also go down by the same rule." The early Mormon convert David Pettigrew rejoiced to find after studying the Book of Mormon that "its gospel was the same and its ordinances were the same as those I had been taught to observe." And his contemporary Joseph Hovey recorded in his journal that his family was baptized only after they "searched the Bible daily" to ensure that it corroborated Book of Mormon teachings.

Many of these converts were seekers or restorationists who were specifically looking for a church that replicated the forms and practices of New Testament Christianity. In the Book of Mormon, they thought they found core doctrines that constituted something closer to the original New Testament gospel than what they were seeing in contemporary churches.

One of the first critics of the Book of Mormon was the Disciples of Christ founder, Alexander Campbell. Many of his congregants were among the first to respond positively to early Mormon missionary work; the similarity of their beliefs eased the transition. So similar were they, in fact, that Campbell accused Smith of stealing his doctrine. As a "reforming" Baptist, for example, Campbell's colleague Walter Scott emphasized five cardinal doctrines of the "Gospel Restored," which would also be the core doctrines of Joseph Smith's "Restored Gospel": "faith, repentance, and baptism for the remission of sins." To this Scott added the gift of the Holy Spirit and the granting of Eternal Life. Smith dropped the fifth as a first principle, and preferred to call the fourth the gift of the Holy Ghost.

The Book of Mormon replicates this presentation of the gospel, in both style and content. Nephi teaches that simplicity is a key concomitant of truth. The apostasy that he prophesies will occur after the Savior's earthly ministry is, in his mind, synonymous with the corruption or excision of "the plain and precious things" essential to the Bible's core message. "Plain" and "plainness" are words he uses some two dozen times as descriptive of the truth, of the word of God, of God's dealings with mankind, and of Nephi's own mode of teaching and prophesying. He does in fact "glory in plainness," and his "soul delighteth in plainness" (2 Ne. 33:6, 25:4, 31:3).

When Nephi distills the essence of the "doctrine of Christ" into plain and simple language, it reduces to the same core principles we saw in Campbell, Scott, and Joseph Smith (not to mention, originally, in the Epistle to the Hebrews 6:1–2). Nephi's version reads:

Wherefore, I would that ye should remember that I have spoken unto you concerning that prophet which the Lord showed unto me, that should baptize the Lamb of God, which should take away the sins of the world. And now, if the Lamb of God, he being holy, should have need to be baptized by water, to fulfil all righteousness, O then, how much more need have we, being unholy, to be baptized, yea, even by water! ... Wherefore, after he was baptized with water the Holy Ghost descended upon him in the form of a dove.... And again, it showeth unto the children of men the straitness of the path, and the narrowness of the gate, by which they should enter, he having set the example before them.... For the gate by which ye should enter is repentance and baptism by water; and then cometh a remission of your sins by fire and by the Holy Ghost.... And now, my beloved brethren, after ye have gotten into this strait and narrow path, I would ask if all is done? Behold, I say unto you, Nay; for ye have not come thus far save it were by the word of Christ with unshaken faith in him, relying wholly upon the merits of him who is mighty to save. Wherefore, ye must press forward with a steadfastness in Christ, having a perfect brightness of hope, and a love of God and of all men. Wherefore, if ye shall press forward, feasting upon the word of Christ, and endure to the end, behold, thus saith the Father: Ye shall have eternal life. And now, behold, my beloved brethren, this is the way; and there is none other way nor name given under heaven whereby man can be saved in the kingdom of God. And now, behold, this is the doctrine of Christ. (2 Ne. 31:4–21)

And so we will find in the Book of Mormon not just an awareness of Christ among this people, but a number of sermons, stories, and epistles, whose teachings are generally consistent with the preaching and letters of Paul.

We have seen how, by visions and revelations, the Nephites learned of the coming of Jesus Christ, and from King Benjamin that faith in Christ was efficacious long before his advent. In one striking instance, a "brother of Jared" living in the era of the Tower of Babel exhibits such unprecedented faith that Christ cannot keep him "from within the veil, therefore he saw Jesus and he did minister unto him" (Ether 3:19). (This unnamed "brother of Jared" belongs to a race of Jaredites, whose migration to the New World, history, and extinction are recounted by Moroni as a tragic precursor to the Nephites' own history, near the end of the Book of Mormon.) Book of Mormon peoples are specifically enjoined to exercise faith in "the Holy One of Israel," whom they elsewhere identify as the incarnate Messiah or "Christ" (2 Ne. 6:9; Omni 1:26). As in the New Testament, miracles and conversions frequently follow upon the exercise of faith that resides in Christ. The captive missionaries Alma and Amulek receive strength to break their bonds "according to [their] faith which is in Christ" (Alma 14:26); the repentant anti-Christ Zeezrom is miraculously healed "according to his faith which is in Christ" (Alma 15:10); angels minister daily to the chief judge Nephi, "for so great was his faith on the Lord Jesus Christ" (3 Ne. 7:18), and so forth. As in biblical accounts of Christ among the gentiles, the missionary Ammon will even bless a Lamanite woman for her faith that exceeds anything seen "among all the people of the Nephites" (Alma 19:10).

Repentance is hardly particular to the New Testament. Generations of Israelite prophets inveighed against faithlessness, wickedness, and idolatry. In the Book of Mormon as well, prophets and missionaries pronounce against a panoply of sins—but they have their own leitmotifs as Jeremiah had his. Nephi decries dwindling faith in spiritual gifts and in the principle of revelation. Jacob, like Paul, emphasizes sexual immorality, placing such a premium on chastity and fidelity that he makes the remarkable promise that, their myriad sins notwithstanding, the Lamanite faithfulness to their wives assures their survival as a people while the otherwise favored Nephite nation will perish utterly (Jac. 3:6). But the sin most reviled in the Book of Mormon is probably pride— usually precipitated by prosperity (though learning runs a close second as cause).

Nephi points the finger of condemnation at "the wise, and the learned, and they that are rich, who are puffed up because of their learning, and their wisdom, and their riches—yea, they are they whom he despiseth" (2 Ne. 9:42; cf. 2 Ne. 28:15). Nephi's successor reaffirms this linkage: "because some of you have obtained more abundantly than that of your brethren ye are lifted up in the pride of your hearts" (Jac. 2:13). Meanwhile, the pattern is repeated among the Lamanites, who "began to increase in riches, and . . . wax great, and began to be a cunning and a wise people, as to the wisdom of the world, yea, a very cunning people, delighting in all manner of wickedness" (Mos. 24:7). The fall into material idolatry brings divine reprimand and affliction, followed by repentance and relief. But the cycle repeats again and again, even among the elect. Alma and his fellow priests "beheld with great sorrow that the people of the church began to be lifted up in the pride of their eyes, and to set their hearts upon riches" (Alma 4:8). He embarks on a preaching crusade with riches and pride as his principal theme. Time and again, righteousness brings prosperity in its wake, only for the blessing to become an occasion for renewed sin. Throughout the tumultuous centuries, we read the recurrent moral that "exceedingly great pride . . . had gotten into the hearts of the people; and it was because of their exceedingly great riches and their prosperity" (Hel. 3:36.) The wild swings from affluence and complacency to repentance and spiritual renewal parallel the recurrent cycles of apostasy and tribulation, repentance and deliverance, which characterize Israel under the Judges. The difference is that in the final years of Nephite existence, when bloodlust combines with pride, they suffer apocalypse rather than renewal.

Baptism receives less attention in the Book of Mormon but enough to situate it firmly in the religious practices of the Nephite people. In transcribing scriptures from the brass plates onto his own, Nephi even records Isaiah as clarifying the expression "waters of Judah" with the words, "or . . . waters of baptism." Other than this allusion, and its inclusion in Nephi's sermon cited earlier, the practice receives no mention until the signal event in Nephite history when Alma the Elder defects from a corrupt court, gathers a group of proselytes in the wilderness, and institutes baptism among his flock. He does not, like Nephi, identify the ordinance with a specific commandment or form of *imitatio Christi*. Rather, he teaches it as a sign that one is entering into a covenant "to mourn with those that mourn; yea, and comfort those that stand in need of comfort, and to stand as witnesses of God at all times and in all things, ... [to] serve him and keep his commandments" (Mos. 18:9–10).

At the end of the Book of Mormon, the editor Moroni will add an epistle from his father Mormon on the subject of infant baptism, which he condemns in the strongest terms as "mockery before God":

> Little children need no repentance, neither baptism. Behold, baptism is unto repentance to the fulfilling the commandments unto the remission of sins. But little children are alive in Christ, even from the foundation of the world; if not so, God is a partial God, and also a changeable God, and a respecter to persons; for how many little children have died without baptism! ... Behold I say unto you, that he that supposeth that little children need baptism is in the gall of bitterness and in the bonds of iniquity; for he hath neither faith, hope, nor charity.... (Moro. 8:11–14)

One hallmark of the New Testament Church is the prominent role assigned the Holy Ghost, which descends at Christ's baptism, is manifest at Pentecost, and bestows a profusion of spiritual gifts described in Acts and the Epistles. Nephi similarly describes the principal function of that Spirit as that of testator of the Messiah "from the beginning of the world until this time, and from this time henceforth and forever" (1 Ne. 12:18), and Jacob recounts the Spirit's manifestation in the form of a dove at the Savior's baptism. The Spirit is linked by Book of Mormon prophets with spiritual rebirth and the baptism of fire, and is associated by them with

Christ and the Father in a triadic formulation. The world of the Book of Mormon, especially after the establishment of the church by Alma, abounds with spiritual gifts. Alma refers to the people of God enjoying "many gifts, the gift of speaking with tongues, and the gift of preaching, and the gift of the Holy Ghost, and the gift of translation" (Alma 9:21). And finally, Moroni, as we saw earlier, rounds out his record and testimony with a promise that all who read his words can know of their truthfulness, and, in fact, ascertain the truth of all things, "by the power of the Holy Ghost" (Moro. 10:5).

The Fortunate Fall

The Book of Mormon can be comfortably familiar in its exposition of basic Christian teachings, like the doctrine of Christ. But it presents strikingly novel doctrines as well. Perhaps the most unusual idea is that of the Fortunate Fall. That expression (*felix culpa*), deriving from a special Easter portion (the Exsultet) of the Latin Mass, was taken by Christians to mean that Adam's sin, the catastrophic consequences of which were inherited by the entire human family, was fortunate insofar as the infinite perfidy of man called forth the infinite goodness of Christ. Sin and betrayal were the catalyst for the universe's most sublime and supernal gesture of deity—God the Son's willing suffering, degradation, and death.

The Book of Mormon goes much further in depicting the Fall as fortunate. The eating of the forbidden fruit is a cause for celebration, not for what it makes manifest through Christ but for what it makes possible in man. While the Fall of man was unquestionably a cosmic tragedy in some sense, the tantalizing question has remained: What would have happened if Adam and Eve had not taken that step? Lehi provides an answer to his sons:

> Behold, if Adam had not transgressed he would not have fallen, but
> he would have remained in the garden of Eden. And all things which

were created must have remained in the same state in which they were after they were created; and they must have remained forever, and had no end. And they would have had no children; wherefore they would have remained in a state of innocence, having no joy, for they knew no misery; doing no good, for they knew no sin. But behold, all things have been done in the wisdom of him who knoweth all things. (2 Ne. 2:22–24)

In this radical recasting of Judeo-Christianity's most foundational myth, the Fall is not a catastrophe to be fixed or rectified, it is the necessary and glorious pathway to humanity's eternal advancement. Simply put, "Adam fell that men might be; and men are, that they might have joy" (2 Ne. 2:25).

The Book of Mormon does little to address the conundrum of how disobedience could be divinely intended and pre-approved, as it were, rather than a wrong turn or detour in the heavenly roadmap. But the Book of Mormon is consistent in reinterpreting the consequences of the choice of Adam and Eve according to this new paradigm. Clearly it would make little sense for God to summarily expel man and woman from Paradise for making a choice so necessary to their happiness. And so, in a way that inverts the normal interpretation of their expulsion, while still according with the letter of the Genesis text, the Book of Mormon redefines that banishment as mercy rather than retribution. For since Adam and Eve have willfully acquired the burden of sin, the Tree of Life now represents the mechanism of immortalizing that fallen nature, making it a curse not a blessing. Alma will make the point twice, that "if Adam had put forth his hand immediately, and partaken of the tree of life, he would have lived forever" (Alma 42:5). Accordingly, he and Eve "would have been forever miserable, having no preparatory state" (Alma 12:26). Instead, "there was a space granted unto man in which he might repent; therefore this life became a probationary state; a time to prepare to meet God; a time to prepare for that endless state which has been spoken of" (Alma 12:25).

The theological repercussions of this revisionism are hard to overestimate. Eve becomes in this scenario the bold heroine, rather than the weak vessel, of the race's founding story. This theme of Eve as happy provocateur finds reinforcement in a later LDS scripture, according to which "Eve, [Adam's] wife, heard all these things and was glad, saying: Were it not for our transgression we never should have had seed, and never should have known good and evil, and the joy of our redemption, and the eternal life which God giveth unto all the obedient" (Moses 5:11, *Pearl of Great Price*). The fall into sin becomes not a shameful episode that reflects and perpetuates an innate depravity, but a necessary immersion into a world of polarities, extremes, and a vitally necessary "opposition in all things." And perhaps most subtle but important, God's observation that "man is become as one of us" is stripped of the divine dismay suggested by the Mosaic account (Gen. 2:22) and recast as something more like sober—even satisfied—recognition.

Atonement

The great Christian mystic William Law wrote that "the whole Nature of the Christian Religion stands upon these two great Pillars, namely, the Greatness of our Fall, and the Greatness of our Redemption." The theological principle underlying human redemption has historically been atonement, the vicarious sacrifice of Jesus Christ, his payment of a debt that ransoms humankind from the penalty of sin and broken law. Even though men and women do not inherit sin or guilt according to the Book of Mormon, they are inevitably liable to both through personal volition. So while the Book of Mormon rejects the traditional understanding of the Fall, it proclaims and elaborates a fairly conventional doctrine of redemption. At least, much of the terminology is conventional, though the Book of Mormon situates the doctrine in a context that endows human agency with special and unambiguous value.

The logic behind Christ's necessary death on the cross on behalf of mankind has taken various forms in Christian thought, but a central theme has treated it as a necessary payment to Justice, in substitution for man's punishment (a view first fully articulated by St. Anselm). The infinite evil of sin against perfect Goodness necessitated an infinite punishment, which only a sinless being could effect. The question of why sin requires punishment in the first place is asked by Alma the Younger's son Corianton, who is troubled "concerning the justice of God in the punishment of the sinner" (Alma 42:1). But while the punishment of a sinner can be reconciled with justice, it is not clear how substitution of an innocent victim can be. This is readily apparent if human standards can in any way point to or illuminate eternal laws. Anyone can satisfy a monetary debt, because a fifty-dollar credit has a positive value that is commensurate with, and therefore cancels out, a fifty-dollar debt. It is based on mathematical equivalence, not justice. To compare a vicarious human sacrifice to the repayment of someone else's debt suggests fearful implications. Analogies to ransom and debt, as Nietzsche pointed out a century ago, work best in a paradigm where the spectacle of punishment provides a pleasure commensurate with the pain caused by the offense, and so cancels the sin, in the same way that a fifty-dollar credit cancels out that fifty-dollar debt. The Book of Mormon provides additional context for interpreting this most difficult of Christian doctrines.

The Book of Mormon has much to say about atonement, forms of the word appearing some three dozen times (it appears once in the KJV New Testament). Through a number of sermons and discourses, Book of Mormon prophets elaborate a doctrine of atonement that incorporates principles of justice and mercy into a framework where moral agency is paramount. In Lehi's sermon on the atonement, he asserts a fundamental dichotomy in the universe between those entities that have agency ("things that act") and those that do not ("things acted upon"). (In a subsequent revelation, Joseph Smith would define the first category as the only true existence: "All truth is independent in that sphere in which God has placed it, to act for itself, as all intelligence also; otherwise there is no existence" [Doctrine & Covenants 93:30].) Such agency, to be efficacious, must operate in the presence of alternatives: "Wherefore, man could not act for himself save it should be that he was enticed by the one or the other" (2 Ne. 2:16). But more to the point, genuine moral agency must entail necessary consequences. If choice is to be more than an empty gesture of the will, more than a mere pantomime of decision-making, there must be an immutable guarantee that any given choice will produce the natural consequence of that choice. In that sense, choice must be choice *of something*. It is the certainty of punishment and reward, defined and differentiated by law and freely chosen by man, that establishes his moral agency.

Christ, Lehi explains, institutes the terms whereby those consequences are assured, and himself stands as the ultimate Guarantor of the integrity of such meaningful choice. As Alma writes, "there is a law given, and a punishment affixed, and a repentance granted; which repentance, mercy claimeth, otherwise justice claimeth the creature and executeth the law" (Alma 42:22). Lehi had made clear that this justice was no transcendent abstraction, no Platonic absolute or universal that held sovereign sway over God himself, but the articulation of cause and effect, choice and consequence, according to laws that Christ himself enunciated, and which established a moral universe predicated upon predictable principles rather than caprice: "Wherefore, the ends of the law [are those] which the Holy One hath given, unto the inflicting of the punishment which is affixed, which punishment that is affixed is in opposition to that of the happiness which is affixed" (2 Ne. 2:10). In this view, Justice seems to be another name for the moral order as defined and implemented by "the Holy One."

Alma is even more explicit in defining "Justice" as a moral order that validates human agency. "The plan of restoration," as he calls this principle, "is requisite with the justice of God; for it is requisite that all things should be restored to their proper order" (Alma

41:2). And how is that order defined? "And if their works were good in this life, and the desires of their hearts were good, that they should also, at the last day, be restored unto that which is good. And if their works are evil they shall be restored unto them for evil" (Alma 41:3–4). But God is also merciful, and if humans can remit a penalty out of compassion or mercy, why cannot God?

Because, Alma continues, such apparent generosity would undermine the essence of that agency on which moral freedom depends. Consequences are chosen at the time when actions are freely committed. To choose to indulge a desire is to choose its fruit—bitter or sweet—assuming, as Lehi did, that "men are instructed sufficiently" to understand what they are choosing (2 Ne. 2:5). Under those conditions, Lehi concludes, "men are free according to the flesh; and all things are given them which are expedient unto man. And they are free to choose liberty and eternal life, through the great Mediator or all men, or to choose captivity and death" (2 Ne. 2:27).

So following the exercise of such agency, "the one [must be] raised to happiness according to his desires of happiness, or good according to his desires of good; and the other to evil according to his desires of evil" (Alma 41:5). It is a truth that harks back to Dante's grim vision of hell, in which God is not even present as Judge or dispenser of punishments, because choices are allowed, inexorably, to bear their own fruit. In Alma's Inferno as well, future states are chosen, not assigned: "For behold," says Alma, "they are their own judges" (Alma 41:7).

The rationale behind such a moral order is not an omnipotent, impersonal, and cruelly inflexible Absolute called Justice, but rather the protection of a necessary framework for human agency which, assuring the promise of righteous reward for the righteous, must equally guarantee evil (whatever is "contrary to the nature of God" [Alma 41:11]) to those who demonstrate through their actions their choice of evil. Given this framework, Alma emphasizes, Corianton's attribution of punishment to a vindictive God is misplaced: "And now, there was no means to reclaim men from this fallen state, *which man had brought upon himself* because of his own disobedience" (Alma 42:12, emphasis mine).

Within these parameters that Lehi and Alma have framed, there can be no escape from the consequences of law without destroying the entire moral order of the universe and both the human agency it grounds and the status of the divine Guarantor of the whole system ("God would cease to be God"). As long as the penalty is executed, law is safeguarded. If a person *chooses* to undo the effects of his decisions and then chooses anew (repentance), agency is safeguarded. So Christ, in a gesture of infinite mercy, offers himself a ransom to the demands of law, as the only being capable of paying a cumulative penalty as "eternal as the life of the soul" (Alma 42:16). Or as the Book of Mormon prophet Amulek writes, "There can be nothing which is short of an infinite atonement which will suffice for the sins of the world" (Alma 34:12). The consequence of unrighteous choice unfolds as it must, but the pain that such choice does (and in this system, must) inflict is voluntarily assumed by a perfect and sinless being. So "justice exerciseth all his demands, and also mercy claimeth all which is her own; and thus, none but the truly penitent are saved" (Alma 42:24).

PART II
The coming forth
of the Book
# of Mormon

Chapter 6

The Book of Mormon and its audiences

The status and meaning of a text is conditioned by the audience to whom it is addressed. But those audiences shift with time. Psalms of praise to God are inspiring as literary instances of adoration, or as they are personally appropriated, made one's own in worshipful reading. Paul's letters, written to specific congregations, had particular authority and efficacy for those intended audiences and, by extension, for Christian communities ever since who embrace the universalism of God's inspired word. In related fashion, the Book of Mormon constructs an audience that shifts its definition with time, eventuating in a carefully constructed bridge to the modern reading public.

When Nephi addresses a reading audience directly, that audience is at first undefined. "I would that ye should know" of his father's faithfulness, he writes only eighteen verses into his record, and then a few verses later, "I will show unto you that the tender mercies of the Lord are over all those whom he hath chosen" (1 Ne. 20). But not until near the end of his record does he specify more exactly whom he has in mind. In the midst of his borrowings from Isaiah, he writes that he is sending his writings "forth unto all my children" (2 Ne. 11:2). Then Nephi follows up with almost one hundred direct addresses to "my people," "you, my children," and "my beloved brethren." Clearly, he has in mind that he is writing a family history to be read by his descendents.

When the Gentile peoples (or non-Israelites) are referred to, as they are dozens of times, it is always in the third person. In one exception, Nephi foresees the Gentiles mocking the Book of Mormon ("We have got a Bible") and turns his prophetic fury on them in an extended apostrophe (2 Ne. 29). Even then, the abrupt transition from "do they remember" to "O ye Gentiles" reveals the direct address as rhetorical, not literal. He immediately goes back to "you," i.e., my brethren, another seventy-some times. From first to last, then, in spite of occasional intimations of a larger, future audience, Nephi has his posterity in mind. As he bears final witness, he prays that his words will "be made strong unto them." Seen in this light, his final farewell to "my beloved brethren, and also Jew, and all ye ends of the earth" is formulaic (2 Ne. 33:4,10). Nephi is writing to Nephites.

The first hint of a transition in the Book of Mormon's intended audience occurs with Nephi's brother and successor Jacob. He praises the Lamanites for their chastity and perceives that because of this "the Lord God will not destroy them" (Jac. 3:6). By contrast, he warns the wicked Nephites that they "may bring [their] children unto destruction" (3:10).

The sense that the originally intended audience may not be around long enough to profit from this record intensifies with Enos, who prays that "if . . . the Nephites, should . . . be destroyed, that the Lord God would preserve a record of . . . the Nephites . . . that it might be brought forth at some future day unto the Lamanites" (Enos 1:13). By the time his son Jarom writes, the writing on the wall is all too apparent. While dutifully maintaining the family genealogy, Jarom simply assumes that he is really writing for "the benefit of our brethren the Lamanites," though he still uses the first person plural (1:2).

His son Omni operates under the new assumption that the Nephites will be no more than a distant memory to futurity, finding it necessary to explain to his distant audience that "the

Nephites" are "[his] people" and indicating that the Lamanites are "their enemies," rather than simply referring to "us" and "our enemies" (Omni 1–2). His son Amaron likewise refers to the Nephites as "them" (6–7), and in the next writer Amaleki's longer narrative the Nephites have become entirely third person, even though he is writing an account of contemporary events. So the transformation of both voice and audience in the small plates of Nephi is now complete. We have gone from "I, Nephi," speaking of "we Nephites," and writing to and for the benefit of "my people, a remnant of the House of Israel, my brethren and my children," to "I Amaleki," speaking of "those Nephites," and doing so "for the benefit of the Lamanites."

In the space of a scant 140 pages, the Book of Mormon has evolved from a family history directed to the clan's posterity, to something more like a last will and testament that preserves a cultural memory and experience for an altogether different audience—the Lamanites. We have no more record of any chronicler addressing a future audience for almost five hundred years—eclipsed as all narrative voices are by the fourth-century editor Mormon. He will intrude into his own narrative only some dozen times over the next three hundred pages, rather like a Victorian novelist, sometimes to emphasize a principle we may miss ("I would that ye should see" or "I would that ye should understand"), sometimes to introduce more thematic unity ("as I said unto you") and sometimes to affirm the moral teleology of his narrative ("I will show unto you" or "in the end of this book ye shall see").

Just whom Mormon is addressing in his direct invocations of audience is not at first clear to the modern reader. Mormon's audience, it turns out, took shape as a result of the visit of the post-resurrection Christ to the Nephites. On that occasion, Christ indicates that the record of the Nephites is destined to be read by a future remnant of Israel, but that it will reach them through the Gentiles, serving as intermediaries. Nephi's earlier quoting of Isaiah foreshadowed this theme: "I will lift up my hand to the

Gentiles, and set up my standard to the people; and they shall bring thy sons in their arms" (1 Ne. 21:22). Mormon records Christ at the time of his visit as commanding the Nephite record-keepers "that ye shall write these sayings" adding that they "shall be manifested unto the Gentiles, *that through* the fulness of the Gentiles, the remnant of [Israel's] seed ... may be brought in." (3 Ne. 16:4; emphasis added).

By the conclusion of Christ's visit to the Nephites, Mormon seems to digest the significance of all this for the audience of the record he is administering. Responding to two facts in particular—the appointed mission of the future Gentiles to provide a conduit (the Book of Mormon) for reestablishing the covenant with Israel, and the approaching destruction of his own people—Mormon now addresses an audience far broader than either the Nephite posterity of Nephi or the Lamanite remnant invoked by Jarom and his successors. Mormon now addresses himself to "ye Gentiles" in earnest, not in rhetorical impatience as Nephi had. At the same time, he recognizes the eventual, *intended* audience as "the remnant of the House of Jacob" (4 Ne. 1:49). He commonly addresses both from this point on, as in Mormon 3:17, 20: "I write unto you, Gentiles, and also unto you, house of Israel, ... yea, behold, I write unto you all." Almost desperate in its outreach, his appeal to futurity antecedes by only a few pages the extermination of that line whom Nephi so consistently and confidently addressed throughout his own narrative. Mormon, in his last words to a distant reader, pleads one last time with the remnant of Israel (identified as the descendents of the Lamanites), knowing full well that if his words even reach them, it will be through the intermediary of a people alien to the house of Israel.

In similar spirit, Moroni takes over the closing pages of the narrative and addresses himself not to a posterity linked to him by bonds of blood or fellow feeling, but to this impersonal, unforeseeable mediator: the vague "he that shall bring this thing to light" or in another anonymous phrase "whoso receiveth this

88

record" (Morm. 8). And then, perhaps resentful of Israel's dependence on such a corrupt vehicle of transmission, having seen in vision the Gentiles' decadence and worldliness, Moroni repeatedly addresses them in urgent reproof and warning, both in an extended address and as he takes them through the narrative of Ether (about the vanished Jaredite civilization). Only in his final chapter does he invoke the Lamanites, the first time we have seen them singled out as an audience since the plates of Nephi. Finally, after his ultimate exhortation to the Gentiles, Moroni signs off with one last, poignant plea for the House of Israel to awake and arise from the dust. Moroni's style is rather like that of a lost explorer, interspersing or embedding messages for loved ones among appeals sent out to unknown rescuers.

We find in the Book of Mormon, then, a clear and consistent shift in audience comprising three phases: a family or tribal history directed to Nephite descendents; the same history directed to their cousins the Lamanites; and a morally tendentious epic directed to remnants of Israel, but having in mind that the narrative will be transmitted to them by a gentile audience—who may or may not be gathered into the House of Israel by adoption. Presumably, those Gentiles equate to the generality of readers of the modern era. What this means is that today's reader of the Book of Mormon begins by reading a narrative of a people distant in time and place, almost as an act of historical eavesdropping. But by the end of the record, the reader has come to realize that the eavesdropper has become in very deed the intended recipient.

Chapter 7
Joseph Smith
and the angel

We have seen that the Book of Mormon may usefully be compared with the Old Testament, insofar as both purport to be sacred narratives beginning as family history that expand into tribal and national history, and encompass religious teachings, sacred prophecies, and potent stories, all recorded by inspired prophets and chroniclers. When it comes to the manner in which these narratives coalesced into a canonical form, acquired sacred status, and assumed their present form and role in religious history, the differences could hardly be more stark. While at least some of the Old Testament is, by general consensus, mythological, and some of its history dubious, much of its history is not. The lands it describes, the nations and personalities who march across its pages, the events it narrates, are in many essentials indisputable as past fact. The Red Sea and the ruins of the Second Temple are still there to see. Cyrus and Nebuchadnezzar were authentic characters of the ancient world. The settlement of Canaan and the fall of Babylon doubtless occurred. A trail of biblical manuscripts extending over two thousand years into the past attest to the Bible itself as a product of an ancient past, however redacted, reworked, and reformulated the final product turned out to be.

Although the Book of Mormon claims to be equally inspired, and to dictate a sacred history every bit as ancient as Kings or Chronicles, virtually nothing associated with the Book of Mormon's origins or

5. Joseph Smith

subject matter can be independently traced with any certainty to a
time earlier than 1827. On the morning of September 23 of that
year, Joseph Smith returned to his parents' home after an all-night
excursion to a nearby hill in the area of Palmyra, New York. Upon
his return, his family described his elation that after four years of
waiting, he had at last been granted stewardship of a set of ancient
plates with the appearance of gold, together with a "key," or set of
"interpreters," to aid in their translation.

Young Smith's history of sacred encounters had begun seven
years earlier, when the fourteen-year-old told his parents and a
few others of a vision reminiscent of Stephen's theophany in
the New Testament. Like the first martyr, Smith saw God the
Father, and Jesus standing on his right hand. Only in the more
recent instance, Smith was alone, praying for religious guidance
in the woods in back of his family farm, and was personally
addressed by the Savior. He was told his sins were forgiven and, in

Box 7.1

Joseph Smith and the angel

While I was thus in the act of calling upon God, I discovered a light appearing in my room, which continued to increase until the room was lighter than at noonday, when immediately a personage appeared at my bedside, standing in the air, for his feet did not touch the floor. He had on a loose robe of most exquisite whiteness. It was a whiteness beyond anything earthly I had ever seen; nor do I believe that any earthly thing could be made to appear so exceedingly white and brilliant.... Not only was his robe exceedingly white, but his whole person was glorious beyond description, and his countenance truly like lightning. The room was exceedingly light, but not so very bright as immediately around his person. When I first looked upon him, I was afraid; but the fear soon left me.

He called me by name, and said unto me that he was a messenger sent from the presence of God to me, and that his name was Moroni; that God had a work for me to do; and that my name should be had for good and evil among all nations, kindreds, and tongues, or that it should be both good and evil spoken of among all people.

He said there was a book deposited, written upon gold plates, giving an account of the former inhabitants of this continent, and the source from whence they sprang. He also said that the fulness of the everlasting Gospel was contained in it, as delivered by the Savior to the ancient inhabitants. (Joseph Smith, History 1:31–34)

response to his prayerful query, that he should not join any extant church.

Three years of heavenly silence followed, along with creeping self-doubt about his spiritual status. In September 1823, the heavens again parted upon his earnest prayers, but this time to reveal a single messenger, clothed in white. He identified himself as Moroni—the same Moroni who completed and buried the sacred record described above—but in resurrected, angelic form. Moroni told Smith that God had work for him to do that would make his name known "for good and evil among all nations." If the first vision had been a personal experience that answered private questions and longings of his heart, this second would launch him into a very public role. If the first revealed him to be a visionary, the second made him a prophet.

The work Moroni outlined involved retrieving, translating, and publishing to the world what he called an account of the former inhabitants of the American continent and "the fulness of the everlasting Gospel ... as delivered by the Savior" to them (JS-H 1:34). Smith, seventeen at the time of this 1823 visitation, was not allowed to actually take possession of the plates until four years had passed, marked by yearly angelic tutorials.

By the time the long anticipated day arrived, Smith had married Emma Hale, who accompanied him to the nearby hill that Moroni had revealed as the site where the plates lay buried. Near the top of the hill, Smith found a stone "of considerable size." He later described his first view of the plates and accompanying artifacts:

> I obtained a lever, which I got fixed under the edge of the stone, and
> with a little exertion raised it up. I looked in, and there indeed did I
> behold the plates, the Urim and Thummim, and the breastplate, as
> stated by the messenger. The box in which they lay was formed by
> laying stones together in some kind of cement. In the bottom of the
> box were laid two stones crossways of the box, and on these stones
> lay the plates and the other things with them.

Some accounts mention two other relics found with the plates: the sword of Laban, which Nephi had brought to the New World, and which became both a model for other weapons and a kingly emblem in its own right, and the Liahona, that spherical brass instrument that functioned as a miraculous compass for Lehi's family during their sojourn in the wilderness.

On the morning that Smith returned home, having at last secured the plates, he seemed to his family and visitors to be much more excited about what the Book of Mormon referred to as the "interpreters," than about the ancient record itself. Eyewitnesses described the instrument, which Smith would later call a "Urim and Thummim," as a pair of crystals set in a figure-eight-shaped silver bow, and attachable to the breastplate by an extending arm or rod. If Smith was initially absorbed by this scrying instrument, through which translated texts and heavenly revelations would appear, his neighbors were more attuned to the gold element in the equation, and the plates quickly became the focus of everyone's attention.

Smith made a few tentative efforts at translating the plates with the help of the interpreters and his wife as scribe, but harassment from locals impeded all his efforts. The pestering was a consequence of several factors: Smith had long been involved in the fad then

6. Hill Cumorah

current in New England of money-digging for lost treasure, and old acquaintances claimed a right to any of his discoveries. Discoveries of Native American artifacts were not uncommon, but a claim to have found precious metal drew unwanted attention. Others apparently responded with hostility to the fantastical claims of a young, apparently delusional or attention-seeking farm boy. Smith interpreted the obstructions as persecution orchestrated by the forces of darkness.

A family friend, Martin Harris, financed Smith's removal to Harmony, Pennsylvania, home of Emma's family. The plates made the trip concealed in a barrel of beans. Isaac Hale allowed the couple refuge on his property, but begrudgingly, given Smith's refusal to let him see the plates at the center of all the commotion. When Smith at last granted permission to eleven friends and relatives to see the plates, Harris, but not Hale, would be among the group. Meanwhile, Harris was having doubts of his own—or at least wanted something in the way of bankable evidence he could present to his wife to justify his investment of time and money in the project. Smith granted permission to take a few transcriptions, along with translations thereof, to a professor of ancient languages at Columbia University in New York City for authentication. In a pattern that perfectly epitomizes Book of Mormon wars to the present day, detractors and believers alike found in the episode clear corroboration of their respective positions.

7. Anthon transcript

Professor Charles Anthon reported after the fact that he immediately saw through the ridiculous hoax, and he warned the New York farmer to dissociate himself from the whole project. Harris said, on the contrary, Anthon affirmed the validity of the translation and wrote an affidavit to that effect. Only upon hearing Harris recount the story of the angel did Anthon retract his signed statement. Anthon maintained his version in two (slightly contradictory) written accounts. Harris, on the other hand, felt confident enough in his understanding of what transpired to throw all his energies behind Smith and even mortgage his property to finance the book's publication. For the next months, he transcribed as Smith dictated the translation.

Enough eyewitnesses to the process of translation left descriptions to piece together some elements, but not all, of how the book was produced. Smith himself gave almost no details. Initially he held the interpreters before his eyes like spectacles as he examined the plates, and dictated to Harris or another scribe (he relied upon several over a period of more than a year) what they revealed. Later, he apparently used a seer stone, which he sometimes employed without the plates even being present. The scribe recorded the words precisely as Smith uttered them, without punctuation or breaks. From late 1827 to June 1828, working with frequent interruptions, Smith dictated a manuscript of 116 pages. Meanwhile, Harris was once again under increasing pressure from his wife to produce hard evidence justifying his role in the venture. He in turn pressured a reluctant Smith to loan him the manuscript, which he finally did, against the express counsel of the Lord (as he later admitted). It was never seen again. Within two weeks, the angel had repossessed the plates and interpreters, Smith's work was gone with nothing to show for it, his role as prophet apparently a colossal failure, his first-born child dead within hours of birth, and his wife at death's door.

Throughout the summer, Smith lingered in shame and uncertainty. Then in September, one year exactly after his initial receipt of the plates, Smith was given a second chance. Lacking

8. Book of Mormon manuscript

both resources and energy, and deprived of Harris's assistance, he resumed translating sporadically. The situation changed dramatically in April 1829, when Oliver Cowdery, a twenty-two-year-old schoolteacher, appeared. Within days, he was won over to the project and working full time as Smith's scribe, while Smith dictated at a prodigious pace. Over the next two months, they churned out something on the order of 3,500 words per day. Cowdery would later reminisce that "These were days never to be forgotten—to sit under the sound of a voice dictated by the inspiration of heaven, awakened the utmost gratitude of this bosom! Day after day I continued, uninterrupted, to write from his mouth, as he translated with the Urim and Thummim, or, as the Nephites would have said, 'Interpreters,' the history or record called 'The Book of Mormon.' "

In June they relocated to the Whitmer family farm in Fayette, New York, where they wrapped up the translation (inserting the redundant account from Nephi's "small plates" to fill the void left by the missing 116 pages of manuscript) and took several important steps forward in the Book of Mormon's history. First, in accordance with allusions made twice in the holy record itself, Smith selected three associates to serve as witnesses to the plates, which until this time had been scrupulously guarded from any eyes but his own. Those men most supportive of his mission were chosen: Oliver the scribe, Martin the (now chastened and repentant) financial backer, and David Whitmer, friend and son in the current host family. Retreating to the woods to pray, the group was at first stymied in their hopes. After Harris recused himself, the three recounted later, an angel appeared to them and displayed the sacred artifacts along with the plates, which he paged through to their astonished view, allowing them to see "and discern the engravings thereon distinctly." Smith found Harris, and together they received the same manifestation.

A few days later, Smith retreated again to the woods with five other members of the Whitmer clan and three from his own where,

9. Oliver Cowdery

devoid of any supernatural voices or angelic presences, he simply presented them with the plates to heft and handle for themselves. All gave their names to affidavits that have been printed with every edition of the Book of Mormon from the first to the present. Subsequently, the three witnesses all defected from Smith and his church (only Whitmer permanently), though all maintained until death the truth of the affidavits.

The next challenge was to get the book into print. The local Palmyra bookseller, E. B. Grandin, at first declined the job—negative media reports had already transformed cool indifference into hostility and opposition on the part of too many potential readers. When Smith initiated arrangements in Rochester instead, the profit motive trumped fear, and Grandin signed a contract—though only after demanding and receiving $3,000 in security. On March 26, 1830, the Book of Mormon was offered for sale in the Palmyra bookstore of E. B. Grandin.

Box 7.2

Witnesses testify about the gold glates

The testimony of three witnesses

" . . . we, through the grace of God the Father, and our Lord Jesus Christ, have seen the plates which contain this record, . . . And we also testify that we have seen the engravings which are upon the plates; and they have been shown unto us by the power of God, and not of man. And we declare with words of soberness, that an angel of God came down from heaven, and he brought and laid before our eyes, that we beheld and saw the plates, and the engravings thereon."

Oliver Cowdery

David Whitmer

Martin Harris

The testimony of eight witnesses

"Joseph Smith, Jun., the translator of this work, has shown unto us the plates of which hath been spoken, which have the appearance of gold; and as many of the leaves as the said Smith has translated we did handle with our hands; and we also saw the engravings thereon, all of which has the appearance of ancient work, and of curious workmanship. And this we bear record with words of soberness, that the said Smith has shown unto us, for we have seen and hefted, and know of a surety that the said Smith has got the plates of which we have spoken. And we give our names unto the world, to witness unto the world that which we have seen. And we lie not, God bearing witness of it."

Christian Whitmer

Hiram Page

Jacob Whitmer

Joseph Smith, Sen.

Peter Whitmer, Jun.

Hyrum Smith

John Whitmer

Samuel H. Smith

PART III

The life and reception of the Book of Mormon

Chapter 8
The Book of Mormon in LDS faith and worship

As we saw above, the doctrine expounded in the Book of Mormon is largely conventional Christian doctrine. Converts found that its Christology, and its emphasis on faith, repentance, baptism, and the Holy Ghost, conformed to their ideas of what Christian scripture should be. What was distinctive about the Book of Mormon had little to do with the theological novelty of its teachings. The significance of the Book of Mormon has been almost entirely bound up not with its content but rather its manner of appearing; it has typically been judged not on the merits of what it *says*, but what it *enacts*. Contemporaries of Joseph Smith described the religious landscape as a "theatre of humbugs," and a "paradise of heterodoxy." New York was especially rife with prophets and crusaders, from Smith's contemporary Matthias the self-proclaimed Messiah to the popular Adventist William Miller and hosts of other seekers and primitivists and restorationists. Expectations of a "new Bible" were rampant, and religious leaders hinted hopefully of angelic heralds who would preach the pristine gospel.

The initial significance of the Book of Mormon was that it distinguished Mormonism as a movement with a discernible difference, and Joseph Smith as a prophet with a testable revelation. Mormon missionary efforts from 1830 to the present have made the Book of Mormon the first link in a chain of interdependent propositions. If the Book of Mormon is a verifiably true revelation from God, the logic runs, then Joseph Smith, its translator and promulgator, must be God's appointed prophet. If that is the case, it justifies Smith's claim to have the authority to restore the priesthood and the church described in the New Testament but subsequently lost through apostasy. Within the Mormon faith, then, the Book of Mormon has operated upon the souls of its adherents primarily by virtue of its status as a sign, an indicator, a signifier rather than a signified. In this capacity as a pointer to meaning outside itself, the Book of Mormon is one of a panoply of heavenly portents that signaled the commencement of a new Christian dispensation. Theophanies, angels, gold plates, Nephite interpreters, magic compasses—the whole entourage of other-worldly visitants and priestly articles were like the vibrant and extravagant uncials in an illuminated manuscript, drawing attention to the inauguration of a new chapter in God's conversation with humankind.

Most of the debates surrounding the Book of Mormon within the Christian community reflect the fact that both believers and skeptics recognize the larger implications of the Book of Mormon's function. For those committed to the integrity and viability of the historical Christian church, no new dispensation or revelation is possible. Similarly, for the majority of Roman Catholics and Protestants alike, committed as they are to the principles of a closed biblical canon and, in the case of the latter, biblical sufficiency (*sola scriptura*), the Book of Mormon is a prima facie challenge and an affront. For those open—or newly converted—to the doctrine that there had been a "falling away" from an original New Testament church and to the ongoing possibility of new prophets and heavenly revelations, the Book of Mormon is the "ensign to the nations," the occasion for a gathering of Israel foretold by Isaiah (Isa. 5:26, KJV).

Consequently, the Book of Mormon continues to be the primary instrument of conversion to the Mormon faith. New members typically trace their religious reorientation, or conversion, to a spiritual witness of the Book of Mormon's truthfulness.

Although the Book of Mormon is generally the catalyst for conversion to the LDS faith, much more than assent to its truthfulness distinguishes Latter-day Saints from other Christians. By the time Smith's life was over, the key doctrines of Mormonism, above and beyond the "doctrine of Christ" found in the New Testament and echoed in the Book of Mormon, would be drawn fromn two additional books of scripture, consisting almost entirely of revelations recorded by Joseph Smith. It is in the *Pearl of Great Price*, and the Doctrine and Covenants, that Mormons largely turn for doctrinal distinctives. Belief in a human pre-mortality, in temples and temple worship, the eternity of the marriage covenant, the distinctive code of health (the Word of Wisdom), the law of tithing, the three-tiered heaven of the afterlife, church offices and organization—these and more besides are to be found in scriptures that add detail and specificity to that restoration of which the Book

Box 8.1

Parley P. Pratt's conversion

"I felt a strange interest in the book. . . . I opened it with eagerness, and read its title page. I then read the testimony of several witnesses in relation to the manner of its being found and translated. After this I commenced its contents by course. I read all day; eating was a burden, I had no desire for food; sleep was a burden when the night came, for I preferred reading to sleep. As I read, the spirit of the Lord was upon me, and I knew and comprehended that the book was true, as plainly and manifestly as a man comprehends and knows that he exists. My joy was now full, as it were, and I rejoiced sufficiently to more than pay me for all the sorrows, sacrifices and toils of my life."

of Mormon serves mainly as portal and witness. At the end of the twentieth century, however, the scripture was coming to assume greater importance in LDS religious life.

A mere two years after the Book of Mormon's publication, Smith delivered a stinging revelation describing the church as "under condemnation" for treating lightly that "new covenant," i.e., the Book of Mormon. If the church began to adopt a more appreciative attitude toward its special scripture, there is little in the historical record to confirm it. Part of the reasons were cultural and part pragmatic. The Mormons drew their converts, as they do today, almost entirely from other Christian denominations. They were therefore immersed in a biblical culture, and still are. They were familiar with King James idiom, and with the doctrines, stories, and language of the Old and New Testaments. Continuing to exploit the cultural grammar they knew would have been largely automatic. Hence, Smith's decision to publish the Book of Mormon in a bible-like binding, to employ Tudor language in all his prophetic translations and pronouncements, and to persist in employing the King James Version of the Bible, even after producing his own "inspired translation" or reworking of it. These choices all attest to a desire to build upon the aura and authority of biblicalism in order to enhance the legitimacy of his work of Christian revisionism.

This also explains why, when Joseph Smith outlined the Church's doctrine and undertook to expound in detail his personal "religious principles" in an 1835 "Letter to the Elders of the Church," he quoted at great length from Luke, Acts, Revelation, Matthew, Isaiah, and Hebrews to teach the fundamentals of repentance, baptism, and the gift of the Holy Ghost. The Book of Mormon received not a mention. Even today, the LDS hymnbook of some four hundred selections has a mere six employing Book of Mormon language or themes. These factors might also explain the failure of the early Latter-day Saints to employ the Book of Mormon more frequently to project a history into which they could inscribe themselves. For example, this uniquely Mormon scripture, this keystone document and American bible, narrates how a close-knit Jewish clan, surrounded by spiritual wickedness and threatened with physical destruction, follow their prophet on a lengthy exodus, at the end of which they discover a promised land, a virtually uninhabited wilderness. There, they raise temples, receive revelations, and become a mighty people and a great nation. Yet when the Illinois Latter-day Saints find themselves surrounded by spiritual wickedness and threatened with physical destruction, follow their prophet on a lengthy exodus, at the end of which they discover a promised land, wherein they will soon rear temples and become a mighty people, it is not to the Book of Mormon but to the Bible that they look for a scriptural precedent for their own unfolding cultural narrative. Pioneers referred to themselves as a modern-day Israel, being led across the plains by a modern Moses (Smith's successor, Brigham Young). And that identification has been thorough and continuous to the present day. True enough, Utah would eventually found her Lehi and her Bountiful, but it is the Jordan River, not the Sidon, that waters the valley, and it was the Camp of Israel, not the Clans of Lehi, that moved across the plains. Old Testament names and places occur some fifteen to twenty times on Utah maps. Book of Mormon sources are confined to three prophets, one city, and a honeybee (Benjamin, Abraham, Bethel, Daniel, Eden, Goshen, Jacob City, Jericho, Jericho Junction, Jerusalem, Jordan, Jordanelle, Moab, Mount Carmel, Ephraim, and Zion vs. Lehi, Nephi, Moroni, Bountiful, and Deseret [the Jaredite word for "honeybee" in the Book of Mormon, and the Mormon name for the Utah Territory]). In the modern era, it would be as late at the 1970s before the church institutionalized the study of the Book of Mormon as part of its Sunday School curriculum. The church school, Brigham Young University, had been requiring its students to study it for only about a decade.

The situation would change dramatically with the inaugural sermon of Ezra Taft Benson upon his succession as church president in 1986. At that time, he warned that the 1832 condemnation was still in force, and made a shift in the Book of Mormon's place in Mormon consciousness and culture the hallmark of his tenure. By 1988 it was clear that Benson had launched the Church into a new era, in which the Book of Mormon received unprecedented attention and respect from Latter-day Saints. In that year, he issued a stirring summons for a "massive flooding of the earth with the Book of Mormon," reaffirmed its role as "the instrument that God designed . . . to gather out [His] elect," and emphatically designated it as of more immediate spiritual relevance and value than the other scriptures. Noting the current churchwide curriculum that apportioned one year of study to every volume of scripture in a four-year sequence, he said: "This four-year pattern, however, must not be followed by Church members in their personal and family study. We need to read daily from the pages of the book that will get a man 'nearer to God by abiding by its precepts, than by any other book.'" In this call for Mormons to "read daily from its pages," it would not be unfair to say that the cultural momentum was building to make the Book of Mormon the principal scriptural focus, not just in missionary efforts but in the Mormon faith tradition generally.

Even in 1972, it was an exaggeration to say, as did Sydney Ahlstrom: "A few isolated individuals can still read [the Book of Mormon] as a religious testimony, . . . but not even loyal Mormons can be nourished by it as they were a century ago." Today, it is simply dead wrong. The Book of Mormon is now the focus of vigorous, scholarly research by Mormon academics that is unprecedented in scope, professionalism, and Church support. The Foundation for Ancient Research and Mormon Studies (FARMS) has a subscribing audience of thousands for its publications on the Book of Mormon. An army of more than fifty thousand missionaries continue to use the Book of Mormon as the centerpiece of a proselytizing effort that was bringing in more than a third of a million converts a year by the new century. In LDS worship services and Sunday Schools, the Book of Mormon is now absolutely central rather than peripheral. Hundreds of thousands of young Mormons daily attend "Early Morning Seminary," a four-year program of gospel study, throughout their high school years. Every participant spends one full year immersed in the "keystone" of their religion, the Book of Mormon. And perhaps most tellingly, Benson's prophetic promises mean that in countless LDS homes throughout the world, devout families meet together every day for a devotional in which they read together from the Book of Mormon. Though Latter-day Saints tend to be extremely Bible-literate, rising generations of their children are more likely to associate scripture reading with the stories of Nephi and Alma than of Matthew and Mark, and to bask imaginatively in the courage of Captain Moroni rather than of Samson or Daniel. Like Muslims, Jews, and other Christians, the Mormons are increasingly coming to be People of the Book—their book.

Chapter 9
Book of Mormon wars

The timing of the Book of Mormon's arrival on the stage of Western Christianity can only be termed ironic. A record claiming to be a literal history of ancient Israelites in America, preserved and translated by supernatural means, appeared on the scene at precisely that moment when the long Christian retreat from biblical literalism was getting under way. The year 1830 saw the Book of Mormon published, the Mormon church established—and the first volume of Charles Lyell's *Principles of Geology* come off the press. Lyell's study, with its meticulous exposition of gradualism and uniformitarianism in geologic history, made a literal reading of Genesis with its six-day creation virtually untenable, paved the way for Darwin, and made higher criticism, with its emphasis on the human rather than divine origins of the Bible, all but inevitable. This was not the best climate in which to introduce another religious record even more steeped in the miraculous, and without the benefit of the veil of historical or geographical distance.

The reception history of the Book of Mormon, therefore, is really two distinct, parallel histories. It is the story of a group of people who were attracted to and galvanized by the palpable evidence of and conduit to heavenly power the book purported to be. That story tells of a pervasive hunger among nineteenth-century religious seekers for signs of God's present workings, of widespread expectations for restoration and return to primitive Christian forms, of a populist passion for egalitarian access to miracles, spiritual gifts, and personal revelation—and how the Book of Mormon met those yearnings. But there is also the story of a protracted debate about the logical plausibility of a book laying claim not just to spiritual value but to actual historical foundations in an ancient American setting, with Israelite characters that seemed wildly out of place and a Christian religion that seemed just as wildly out of its proper time frame. Both stories continue into the new millennium with unabated fervor.

Then, as now, few critics of Mormonism made the effort to actually read and assess the religion's holy scriptures. The sociologist Thomas O'Dea's jibe about not needing to read the Book of Mormon to have an opinion of it was an accurate reflection of the general situation, in which debates seldom engaged with the Book of Mormon's message or theology. It wasn't long, however, before the book caused sufficient stir and made sufficient headway with susceptible converts that critics began to produce theories of its genesis to compete with Smith's official version.

The Book of Mormon addressed a number of issues that struck some observers as suspiciously relevant to contemporary religious debates. In 1832 Alexander Campbell, a competing restorationist, published the first criticism of the work, a pamphlet none too-subtly titled *Delusions*. In it, Campbell characterized the Book of Mormon as a mélange

> of every error and almost every truth discussed in New York for the last ten years. He decided all the great controversies:—infant baptism, ordination, the trinity, regeneration, repentance, justification, the fall of man, the atonement, transubstantiation, fasting, penance, church government, religious experience, the call to the ministry, the general resurrection, eternal punishment, who may baptize, and even the question of free masonry, republican government and the rights of man.

While believers took Joseph Smith's lack of education as evidence that divine inspiration was behind his many-layered work, detractors like Campbell saw it as evidence of hidden collaborators or literary theft. Sidney Rigdon was a well-educated and rhetorically polished ex-Campbellite preacher, and it was he whom Campbell believed had authored the work, incorporating a text supposedly written by one Solomon Spaulding. That hypothesis was later displaced when some parallels were noted with Ethan Smith's 1823 *View of the Hebrews*, one of many contemporary efforts to link the native North Americans to the lost tribes of Israel. The Dominican friar Diego Duran had suggested such a connection in the sixteenth century, and it was picked up by Gregorio Garcia's *Origin of the Indians of the New World* in 1607. English language publications on the subject included Thomas Thorowgood's *Jews in America, or Probabilities That the Americans are of that Race* (1650), which influenced the Puritan John Eliot. Over the next two centuries, popular and influential treatments asserting Israelite ancestry of the American Indians would be produced by James Adair in 1775 and Elias Boudinot in 1816, before Ethan Smith's popular work.

Most critics find the Book of Mormon's parallels to books like *View of the Hebrews* less than persuasive of borrowing, but the search for some influence or complex of influences arising out of Smith's context has continued unabated. Psychologists writing in the 1920s and, a few decades later, Fawn Brodie, author of a critical biography of Joseph Smith, alleged that anti-Masonic fervor, which broke out over the murder of Mason-exposer William Morgan in 1826, led to the depiction in the Book of Mormon of the "Gadianton Robbers." Both were described as a "secret combination," and employed secret oaths in their rituals (though Joseph Smith was himself a supporter and borrower of Masonry, not a critic).

Brodie also saw the influence of anti-Roman Catholicism in the Book of Mormon. In Joseph Smith's youth, the construction of the

Erie Canal led to the influx of enough Irish laborers to stir up resentments in upstate New York, and sporadic attacks on the Catholic Church appear in Rochester papers and the Albany press. So when the prophet Nephi, as recorded in the Book of Mormon, sees in vision a "great and abominable church," "the whore of all the earth," "whose foundation is the devil," Brodie—as have many Mormons—assumed that such images refer to the Roman Catholic Church in a way that recalls St. John's language in the book of Revelation. Finally, Brodie thinks she detects "Calvinism and Arminianism" in the Book of Mormon, though "they had equal status, depending upon which prophet was espousing the cause, and even universalism received a hearing."

More recently, scholars have emphasized early Mormonism as a product of dramatic social change and a resultant social anxiety of the 1820s and 1830s. Some have seen Mormonism as articulating through the Book of Mormon a theocratic refuge from too much pluralism and a Utopian alternative to too much class conflict. (In the reign of the Nephite judges, political and spiritual authority are often combined, and Christ's visit ushers in an era of blissful harmony where racial and social distinctions disappear.) Others have found, as Campbell did earlier, a preoccupation with theological debates over everything from proper liturgical forms to who should have access—and how often—to the Lord's supper. Other partisans of the "environmental approach" to the Book of Mormon believe they have found in the text references to disputes about the contract of works versus the covenant of grace and to competing theories of atonement that were of special concern to nineteenth-century audiences. Book of Mormon condemnation of latter-day libertinism has been interpreted as a veiled attack on the implications of the universalism embraced by so many of Joseph Smith's contemporaries. Finally, it is undeniably the case that folk magic, slippery treasures, and emotionally extravagant reactions to conversion all make their appearance in the Book of Mormon and in the popular culture of Joseph Smith's day.

Mormons were undismayed by the transparent relevance of the Book of Mormon to nineteenth-century cultural and religious preoccupations for two reasons. First, because as Moroni wrote to his future readers, "Jesus Christ hath shown you unto me, and I know your doing" (Morm. 8:35). Mormon readers, in other words, believed the text's ability to engage and clarify contemporary debates was a crucial feature of its inspired nature. Its prescience was evidence of divine foresight. Second, and in a similar way, the enduring and pervasive appeal of the mystery of Amerindian origins only made the Book of Mormon's case more compelling since it claimed to provide a historical, rather than speculative, solution to the conundrum.

In the nineteenth century, when archaeology was in its infancy (Brigham Young University, for example, had no chair in archaeology until 1945), Mormon claims of empirical corroboration in the ruins of Yucatan and Central America went largely uncontested, if also largely ignored. A expedition to Columbia in search of the Nephite capital, Zarahemla, under Brigham Young Academy president Benjamin Cluff, typified the naïve enthusiasm that persisted into the modern era. The year 1921 marked a turning point, when the leading church intellectual B.H. Roberts accepted the task of responding to an outside query about historical implausibilities in the Book of Mormon, and he discovered that these presented genuine challenges to Mormon apologetics. The list of difficulties consisted of apparent anachronisms like steel, silk, scimitars, and horses, along with the immense variety of Indian languages that seemed to belie a single, Hebraic origin.

The latter difficulty, and many kindred problems, is obviated when Mormon scholars embrace an interpretation that sees the Nephites and Lamanites as one immigrant group among many, and inhabiting a greatly restricted geographical area; these assumptions are now the norm. The anthropologist John Sorenson has shifted Mormon interpretation in that direction, arguing for a Mesoamerican setting for the Book of Mormon by collating some seven hundred geographical references in the text. Mormon apologists have responded to other difficulties with varying degrees of success. At the same time, however, the sober realization has long since hit Mormon scholars that historical research into Book of Mormon claims is a two-edged sword.

Still, enthusiasts rush in where scholars fear to tread. Amateur archeologists persisted in research expeditions and publishing projects that could not bear up to critical scrutiny, creating an easy target for professionally trained specialists. Important exceptions to this trend exist. One effort has involved mapping the possible route of Lehi's family through the Arabian wilderness described in the Book of Mormon. Researchers have posited candidates for the River of Lemuel, agree upon a general route along the Incense Trail, and also agree that Lehi's point of departure in the verdant land Bountiful was along Oman's southern coast. Other external approaches to the Book of Mormon's historicity include the use of indirect evidence, like the compilation of massive bibliographies of diffusionist evidence (such as the one by John Sorenson and Martin Raish, who published *Pre-Columbian Contact with the Americas Across the Oceans* [FARMS Research Press, 1996]). More recently, Sorenson has collated an impressive array of biological evidence to the same ends.

Archaeologically, one outspoken critic of the Book of Mormon has scoffed that archaeologists have no more chance of finding evidence of Book of Mormon place names "than of discovering the ruins of the bottomless pit described in the book of Revelations [*sic*]." Yet in the 1990s, a German archaeology team discovered a carved altar a few dozen miles east of modern San'a inscribed with a reference to the tribe of "NHM," and another with a like inscription has since been found from that area. Located in the place where Nephi's record locates Nahom, these altars appear to be the first hard, archaeological evidence for the historicity of the Book of Mormon.

The most recent development in the Book of Mormon wars has been a flurry of claims that DNA evidence proves that there is no genetic link between Native American populations and an Israelite heritage. To the LDS, the DNA approach is a red herring. As one molecular biologist and member of a scientific review panel for the National Science Foundation points out, at least ten factors make the hypothesis of the American Indian–Israelite connection untestable. For instance, the science is difficult of application given the uncertainties about the genetic makeup of the founding pool of the supposed Book of Mormon peoples, and its inevitable genetic contamination during a thousand years of Book of Mormon history and the fifteen centuries since. Book of Mormon scholars have been pointing out for generations that the scripture itself does not claim that the Jaredites or Lehites established or sustained a presence in the utter absence of other indigenous or subsequently arrived groups, though a 1981 introduction to the LDS version of the Book of Mormon implied as much; more to the point, the very word "Lamanite," which critics (aided and abetted by popular LDS usage) take to refer to modern Native Americans, does not in the Book of Mormon denote an ethnic or racial category. Within five hundred years of settlement, the terms Nephite and Lamanite are employed to designate one's religious loyalties (Alma 3:11). Even from a Mormon perspective, in other words, there is no identifiable genetic descendent of Laman or Lemuel to test.

In addition to responding to the theories of environmental influence on the Book of Mormon, LDS apologists have actively promoted a research agenda based more on textual analysis than archaeological researches. One of contemporary Mormonism's greatest intellectuals, Hugh W. Nibley, insisted in the 1940s that the search for external evidence was a misdirection. The question we should be asking of the Book of Mormon is, does it correctly reflect "the cultural horizon and religious and social ideas and practices of the time"? Does it have authentic historical and geographical background? Is the mise-en-scène mythical, highly imaginative, or extravagantly improbable? Is its local color correct, and are its proper names convincing? Until recent years men were asking the same questions of the book of Exodus, and scholars were stolidly turning thumbs down until evidence accumulating in its favor began to turn the scales. As one student described it, the problem "is rather to prove, by innumerable small coincidences, that which Ebers has so well called the 'Egypticity' of the Pentateuch, than to establish any particular historical point by external and monumental evidence." Just so the problem of 1 Nephi is to establish both its "Egypticity" and its "Arabicity" by like innumerable coincidences.

A recent outline of Nibley's work on the Book of Mormon surveys forty-five topics where he finds historical corroboration for Book of Mormon themes, practices, and textual elements. Egyptian etymologies and the word for "honeybee" (deseret), the motifs of luminous stones and dancing princesses in the Book of Ether, the practice of olive culture and of naming geographical features— these and dozens of other topics are shown in Nibley's analyses to be fully congruent with a Middle Eastern setting. He compares Lehi's rhetorical practice with the "qasida," or desert poetry, examines Book of Mormon assemblies in the light of New Year rites described in Old World texts, and finds ancient precedents for unusual phraseology (such as "the cold and silent grave, from whence no traveler can return" and the often mentioned "land of Jerusalem"), and for the book's introductory and concluding style of colophons. He verifies the historical correctness of Nephi's hunting weapons (bows and slings) and finds a striking etymology for the peculiar word "Hermounts," a Book of Mormon wilderness infested with wild beasts. In Egypt he locates a district called Hermonthis, named after Month, the Egyptian god "of wild places and things." Ritual games in which life and limb are forfeit, peculiar rites of execution, and hiding up treasures unto the Lord, all are Book of Mormon elements that find Old World antecedents under Nibley's expansive scholarship.

For all his efforts, Nibley found few to pay attention to his work outside Mormon circles. One prominent scholar of Near Eastern studies, though completely unpersuaded by Smith's angel stories, nonetheless agreed with Nibley that one cannot explain away the presence in the Book of Mormon of genuinely Egyptian names, like Paanchi and Pahoran, in close connection with a reference to the text as written in "reformed Egyptian." Otherwise, Nibley registered little outside impact.

Within the church, his approach has inspired the work of an independent research institute, the Foundation for Ancient Research and Mormon Studies (FARMS), which was formed in 1979 (and has since been incorporated into the Neal A. Maxwell Institute for Religious Scholarship at Brigham Young University). By 1997 the quality of its work was changing the dynamics of Book of Mormon apologetics. Two evangelical scholars acknowledged in a much heralded paper that "in recent years the sophistication and erudition of LDS apologetics has risen considerably . . . [and] is clearly seen in their approach to the Book of Mormon." As difficult as it may be to accept the fact, "LDS academicians are producing serious research which desperately needs to be critically examined," they insisted.

Researchers at FARMS believe they have succeeded in producing "a considerable body of analysis demonstrating that at least something of the strangeness of the Book of Mormon is due to the presence in it of other ancient and complex literary forms which Joseph Smith is highly unlikely to have discovered on his own, and showing as well that its contents are rich and subtle beyond the suspicions of even the vast majority of its most devout readers." As even a determined skeptic admits, it is hard to ignore the "striking coincidences between elements in the Book of Mormon

and the ancient world, and some notable matters of Book of
Mormon style."

Following Nibley's lead, suggesting that the Book of Mormon
should be viewed as a product of Old World cultures rather than a
New World artifact, John Welch first noted how chiasmus, or
inverted parallelism (which we saw earlier), a poetic structure
common in antiquity, turns out to be pervasive in the Book of
Mormon. The form is common in the Bible, in a passage like Isaiah
6:10, for example:

(a) Make the **heart** of this people fat,

      (b) and make their **ears** heavy,

            (c) and shut their **eyes**;

            (c′) lest they see with their **eyes**,

      (b′) and hear with their **ears**,

(a′) and understand with their **heart**....

Though chiasmus is also common, in small doses, to many poets
across time, the examples in the Book of Mormon are at times
remarkably intricate and extensive, as we saw in the case of
Alma 36.

Assessing the plausibility of an Israelite presence in the New
World, some believe they have found direct evidence for such a
connection in linguistic parallels between Semitic and
Uto-Aztecan languages. Several other LDS scholars have focused
on various examples of Hebraic structures in the Book of Mormon,
going beyond the chiasmus discussed earlier to note shared
instances of "if–and" constructions, cognate accusatives, the
construct state, and other examples.

None of these items, of course, taken singly, constitutes decisive
proof that the Book of Mormon is an ancient text. Even their

cumulative weight is counterbalanced by what appear to be striking intrusions into the Book of Mormon text of anachronisms, nineteenth-century parallels, and elements that appear to many scholars to be historically implausible and inconsistent with what is known about ancient American cultures. If the past two centuries is any indication, scholarly analysis will continue do little more than reinforce the conclusions different constituencies already bring with them to the Book of Mormon.

Chapter 10
Conclusion: The Book of Mormon in the twenty-first century

The Book of Mormon is revered as scripture by millions of people. While it has many affinities with the Bible of Christendom, it does not fulfill the same role in the LDS faith that the Bible does in the Christian faith. But it may share one function with other scriptures in world religion: the Book of Mormon is a potent and disruptive text. The Russian theorist Mikhail Bakhtin argued that there are two modes of language by which we are influenced—what he calls authoritative discourse, and internally persuasive discourse. The latter category is any language that makes its claim upon us on the basis of its logic, rhetorical appeal, compelling argument, or emotional sway. "The authoritative word," on the other hand, "demands that we acknowledge it, that we make it our own; it binds us, quite independent of any power it might have to persuade us internally; we encounter it with its authority already fused to it." Some language, in other words, is so wedded to an authoritative source that we find it difficult or impossible to assess the content as content. We cannot analyze, negotiate, critique, or selectively assimilate it.

The Book of Mormon likewise shatters familiar religious paradigms and reconfigures them with a totality that is resistant to compromise. The foregrounding of the book's own provenance, and its historical employment as a sign of Joseph Smith's prophetic calling and authority, have wedded the scripture effectively to questions of Joseph Smith's authority and authenticity. At the same time, the book is an important cultural document of the nineteenth century, evoking a reception by thousands and then millions in a way that has much to tell us about the spiritual sensitivities and the religious yearnings to which it so obviously appealed. The Book of Mormon is, by any measure, a book of rich imagination, narrative complexity, and poetic qualities. It has only been in the last generation that scholars have plumbed the literary richness of the Bible, separate and apart from its revelatory or historic import. A similar move is likely to occur with the Book of Mormon, as Latter-day Saints turn to their signal scripture under the impetus of new prophetic emphases, and non-Mormons turn to examine a book so central to the culture and doctrine of a rapidly growing international church.

That larger context into which the Book of Mormon is entering, with Mormonism's rapid growth in Latin America and Africa, is undoubtedly going to create challenges to the way the Book of Mormon is presented and made relevant. The difficulty may be suggested by what the German philosopher of the Enlightenment G. E. Lessing said in reference to revealed religion generally. "Accidental truths of history," he said, "can never become the proof of necessary truths of reason." If key elements of religious faith are tied to particular times and places in human history, in other words, then access to religious truth is made dependent on happenstance rather than on fixed principles of reason available to all. The historical situatedness of any church's birth, the small geographical compass limiting the world's exposure to it, its particular context in a definite culture and language—all these factors militate against any religion's claim to universal validity. A just God, the argument went, would make sure the gospel was equally accessible to all, with no persons of a particular time or place given a special advantage.

At first glance, Mormonism and its iconoclastic scripture seem a prime embodiment of this problem. "Do you wish to purchase a history of the origins of the Indians?" was the pitch of the first Mormon missionary. The Mormon church's modest beginnings in upstate New York, and early Mormon emphasis on the Book of Mormon's value as a Rosetta stone to the mystery of ancient American civilizations, suggest a geographically and culturally limited appeal. In actual fact, the Book of Mormon resists the Enlightenment critique in ways that may make it well situated to expand its influence in the twenty-first century.

In some ways, it is true, the book has been an intensely American book, with its stories of ancient New World inhabitants, its discovery in New York, its predictions of a New Jerusalem in the Western Hemisphere, and its themes of personal liberty and individualized revelation strongly attractive to antebellum Americans. But the Book of Mormon is also powerfully iconoclastic and inclusivist. If there is any constant thread to the Book of Mormon's invoking and reworking of familiar themes, it is to be found in its pattern of severing the association of God and his favor with any one particular time or place, people or nation. As we saw, the Book of Mormon makes a habit of fracturing biblical themes into endless echoes of an original revelation, of an original covenant, of an original ascension, and of an original Zion. The thematic thrust of the Book of Mormon is to reveal these forms as endlessly replicated across time, across history, and across tribes. For these reasons especially, the Book of Mormon's work of dislocation and decentering may resonate in a twenty-first century world increasingly resistant to old boundaries and the categories of the past.

Appendix: Manuscripts, editions, and translations

The first edition of the Book of Mormon in 1830 consisted of a print run of five thousand copies. John H. Gilbert, the principal compositor at E. B. Grandin's shop where the book was printed, described the first twenty-four pages of manuscript delivered by Joseph's brother Hyrum as "closely written and legible, but not a punctuation mark from beginning to end." Gilbert added punctuation and paragraphing, but no versification. The first edition, like several subsequent ones, therefore looked like a Bible in outer appearance but more like a novel within.

Having lost the first 116 pages of the manuscript, Smith took care to have Oliver Cowdery (with the help of two scribes) produce a printer's copy (P) of the remaining original for typesetting purposes. That manuscript version, virtually entire, is today owned by the Community of Christ, formerly the Reorganized Church of Jesus Christ of Latter Day Saints, the largest of several Restoration movements that defected from the succession of Brigham Young to church leadership. The original Book of Mormon manuscript (O) was deposited by Joseph Smith in the cornerstone of the Nauvoo House in 1841. Subsequently, water damage and dispersal of many of the remaining fragments accounted for the loss of three-quarters of the MS. The balance is today housed in the LDS Historical Department.

Harris bore the financial burden of initial publication and anxiously engaged in the work of hawking the new volumes. Reception hovered between hostile resistance and indifference. Within weeks, Joseph

Knight, who along with the Prophet, encountered Harris loaded down with unsold copies, recorded the famous result of his efforts: "The books will not sell for no Body wants them," the farmer lamented.

Harris's remark was slight overstatement, but it did take seven years before members and missionaries had distributed enough copies to warrant the printing of a second edition, produced in the then church headquarters of Kirtland, Ohio. The print run may have equaled the first, and it incorporated hundreds of changes, mostly grammatical. Smith oversaw a third edition in 1840 (two thousand copies) that corrected many errors based on comparison of the original MS, and the next year some four thousand copies based on the second edition were published in Liverpool, in response to a thriving missionary work in England.

The first edition to incorporate major changes was the 1879 edition, which LDS apostle Orson Pratt edited. He organized the book using the same versification system current in today's editions and added extensive footnotes. Most of those cross-referenced other scriptures, but one innovation he introduced was the keying of Book of Mormon place names to modern geographical counterparts. Zarahemla, in this system, is annotated as "north of the head waters of the river Magdalena ... south of the isthmus" (Omni 1:13).

James E. Talmage supervised the next major edition in 1920. Adopting a more prudent position regarding Book of Mormon geography, he eliminated all geographical footnotes. Double columns and chapter summaries brought the edition to the layout familiar to today's readers. One final development was the 1981 edition, which reworked introductory material and headings, made further corrections based on the original manuscript, and provided a new footnote system that more thoroughly integrated the Book of Mormon with the Bible and other LDS scriptures. A trade edition of the Book of Mormon based on this edition is published by Doubleday, and the University of Illinois Press publishes a *Reader's Edition* of the Book of Mormon based on the 1920 edition. It changes no words, but reformats the text and provides extensive editorial assists to clarify the myriad shifts in authors and narrators, direct and indirect discourse, and to highlight poetic form and thematic structure. A recent development of tremendous scholarly and religious significance to Mormons is the production of a Book of

Mormon critical text, in which Royal Skousen is recuperating an original manuscript to the Book of Mormon, and showing every substantive change made from its original to its present editions. The work is multivolume and ongoing.

Mormon missionaries were spreading their gospel to Canada before the Book of Mormon was even printed, and to England by 1837. Missionary work soon spread to Wales and Western Europe, occasioning the first foreign translation of the Book of Mormon, Danish, in 1851, followed by French, Welsh, German, and Italian versions the following year. By the end of the century, Hawaiian, Swedish, Spanish, Maori, and Dutch had been added. The pace accelerated in the next several decades; ten translations had occurred from 1850 to 1900 while over fifty more were produced by 2000— almost half of those in the last decade of the century as the rate of translation increased dramatically. This pace continues in the new millennium, with more than a dozen full translations in the first five years alone, some of the latest being the Ghanaian language Twi, Yapese of Micronesia, and Indian dialects of Telugu and Tamil. In addition, to expedite the availability of the Book of Mormon abroad, the church began a practice of translating select portions for publication, rendering some forty-four abridgments in the 1970s and 1980s. At the present day, well over one hundred full or partial translations of the Book of Mormon are in print.

Book of Mormon timeline

1820	spring	Joseph Smith experiences his First Vision
1823	Sept.	Angel Moroni appears to Joseph Smith; Smith relates visitation to his family
1824	Sept.	1st annual return of Moroni to Smith
1825	Sept.	2nd annual return of Moroni to Smith
1826	Sept.	3rd annual return of Moroni to Smith
	Nov.	Smith divulges his mission to the Joseph Knight family
1827	Sept.	Smith retrieves the plates from Hill Cumorah
	Dec.	Assisted by family friend Martin Harris, Smiths relocate to Harmony, Pennsylvania, to escape harassment
1828	Feb.	Martin Harris takes sample of Book of Mormon script to Charles Anthon of Columbia College for validation
	June	Smith completes dictation of 116 pages of text, using Harris as scribe. Lends MS to Harris
	summer	Harris loses manuscript. Moroni repossesses plates and interpreters
	Sept.	Moroni restores plates and interpreters to Smith; translation resumes very sporadically, with Emma and Reuben Hale as scribes
1829	March	Smith told by the Lord to desist translating until help should arrive
	April–June	Bulk of translation completed, employing Oliver Cowdery as scribe

	June	Cowdery, Harris, and David Whitmer see and testify to the reality of plates, as the "Three Witnesses"; eight friends and family members do likewise a few days later
	Aug.	Agreement secured with printer E. B. Grandin. Typesetting begins. Harris mortgages farm to secure expense
	fall	First signatures of the book begin to circulate.
1830	March	5,000 copies of the Book of Mormon come off the press
	April	Smith formally organizes the Church of Christ (later the Church of Jesus Christ of Latter-day Saints)

References

Chapter 1

The remark by Thomas O'Dea is from *The Mormons* (Chicago: University of Chicago Press, 1957), 26.

Chapter 2

The "influential theologian" is Emil Brunner, *Our Faith* (New York: Scribner's Sons, 1954), 11–12. The "contemporary religious scholar" is Elizabeth A. Johnson, *She Who Is: The Mystery of God in Feminist Theological Discourse* (New York: Crossroad, 1992), 7. She provides full citations for the passages she quotes.

The definitions of prophecy appear in "Prophecy," *Oxford Dictionary of the Christian Church*, ed. F. L. Cross and E. A. Livingstone (Oxford: Oxford University Press, 1997), 1336; and in Abraham Heschel, *The Prophets* (New York: Harper and Row, 1962), xviii.

The Eusebius quotation is from *The History of the Church from Christ to Constantine*, trans. G. A. Williamson (Middlesex: Dorset, 1983), 3.3, 41. Augustine's statement appears in *Retractions* I.12.3, trans. Mary Inez Brogan (Washington, DC: Catholic University of America Press, 1968), 54. Norman J. Cohen's remarks come from *The Way into Torah* (Woodstock, VT: Jewish Lights Publishing, 2000), 84–85.

Chapter 4

Mark Twain's famous jibe comes from *Roughing It* (Hartford, CT: American Publishing, 1899), 1: 132.

Chapter 5

Remarks of the first-generation converts can be found in "John
Murdock Autobiography," 12, 15, LDS Church Archives; Orson
Pratt, *Deseret News* IX, 153–55; Eli Gilbert, *Messenger and Advocate*
1.1 (October 1824): 10; the David Pettigrew journal and the journal
of Joseph Hovey are both in Special Collections, Harold B. Lee
Library, Brigham Young University.

On the Campbellite "Gospel Restored," see Winfred Ernest Garrison
and Alfred T. DeGroot, *The Disciples of Christ: A History* (St. Louis:
Bethany, 1958), 188. William Law's statement is from "Of the Nature
and Necessity of Regeneration," in *Works* (London 1763), 5:56.

Chapter 7

Joseph Smith describes his retrieval of the gold plates in an account
canonized as LDS scripture, in Joseph Smith-History 1:52, *Pearl of
Great Price* (Salt Lake City: Church of Jesus Christ of Latter-day
Saints, 1981). Oliver Cowdery recounted his experience as translator
in *Messenger and Advocate*, 1.1 (October 1834): 15.

Chapter 8

The account of Pratt's conversion comes from the *Autobiography of
Parley P. Pratt*, edited by his son, Parley P. Pratt (Salt Lake City:
Deseret Book Co., 1985), 20. Ezra Taft Benson's summons to the LDS
church appears in "Flooding the Earth with the Book of Mormon,"
Ensign 18.11 (November 1988): 4–5. His words on Book of Mormon
study borrow from Joseph Smith, *History*, 4: 461. Sydney Ahlstrom's
misperception appears in his *Religious History of the American
People* (New Haven: Yale University Press, 1972), 504.

Chapter 9

Alexander Campbell's attack on the Book of Mormon was published as
Delusions: An Analysis of the Book of Mormon (Boston: Benjamin
H. Greene, 1832), 85. For Fawn Brodie on the Book of Mormon, see
*No Man Knows My History: The Life of Joseph Smith the Mormon
Prophet*, 2nd ed. (New York: Vintage Books, 1995), 59, 62–66, 70,
413–17. The dismissal of Book of Mormon archaeological evidence

comes from Michael Coe, "Mormons and Archaeology: An Outside View," *Dialogue: A Journal of Mormon Thought* 8.2 (Winter 1973): 48. Michael Whiting assesses the DNA controversy in "DNA and the Book of Mormon: A Phylogenetic Perspective," *Journal of Book of Mormon Studies* 12.1 (2003): 24–35. The approach to Book of Mormon apologetics described by Hugh W. Nibley appears in his *Lehi in the Desert*, in *The Collected Works of Hugh Nibley* (Provo, UT: Deseret and FARMS, 1988), 5:4. The scholar intrigued by the Book of Mormon's Egyptian etymologies was William F. Albright, writing to Grant S. Heward (July 25, 1966) and cited in John A. Tvedtnes, John Gee, and Matthew Roper, "Book of Mormon Names Attested in Ancient Hebrew Inscriptions," *Journal of Book of Mormon Studies* 9.1 (2000): 45. The appraisal of Carl Mosser and Paul Owen on Book of Mormon scholarship is from "Mormon Apologetic, Scholarship, and Evangelical Neglect: Losing the Battle and Not Knowing It?" *Trinity Journal* (1998): 181, 185, 189. The FARMS self-appraisal appears in Daniel C. Peterson, "Editor's Introduction: By What Measure Shall We Mete?" in *FARMS Review of Books* 2 (1990): xxiii. The concession of the skeptic is from David P. Wright, " 'In Plain Terms that We May Understand': Joseph Smith's Transformation of Hebrews in Alma 12–13," in Brent Lee Metcalfe, ed., *New Approaches to the Book of Mormon*, (Salt Lake City: Signature, 1993), 165 n.

Chapter 10

The first known missionary pitch, of Samuel Smith, is recorded in Lucy Mack Smith, *History of Joseph Smith by His Mother* (Salt Lake City: Stevens and Wallis, 1945), 169.

The Mikhail Bakhtin quotation is from "Discourse in the Novel," *The Dialogic Imagination: Four Essays*, ed. Michael Holquist (Austin: University of Texas Press, 1981), 42. The passage from Lessing is in G. E. Lessing, "On the Proof of Spirit and Power," in *The Christian Theology Reader*, 3rd ed., Alister E. McGrath, ed. (Oxford: Blackwell, 2007), 296. Gilbert's description of the Book of Mormon manuscript can be found in his letter to James T. Cobb, February 10, 1879, in Dan Vogel, ed., *Early Mormon Documents* (Salt Lake City, UT: Signature, 1998), 2: 522–23. Martin Harris's despondent remark to Joseph Knight is documented in Dean Jessee, "Joseph Knight's Recollection of Early Mormon History," *BYU Studies* 17.1 (Autumn 1976): 36–37.

Further reading

Bushman, Richard L. *Mormonism: A Very Short Introduction.*
  New York: Oxford University Press, 2008. An elegant and concise
  overview of Mormonism by the foremost historian in the field.
Givens, Terryl L. *By the Hand of Mormon: The American Scripture
  that Launched a New World Religion.* New York: Oxford
  University Press, 2002. A reception study with an emphasis on the
  various functions the scripture has fulfilled in the LDS faith
  tradition.
Hardy, Grant, ed. *The Book of Mormon: A Reader's Edition.* Urbana:
  University of Illinois Press, 2003. An unabridged version of the
  Book of Mormon, but employing frequent headings and formatting
  for greater clarity and ease of use than the official LDS edition,
  with special attention to its narrative complexity.
Metcalfe, Brent Lee. *New Approaches to the Book of Mormon:
  Explorations in Critical Methodology.* Salt Lake City, UT:
  Signature Books, 1993. A collection of essays that contest the
  ancient origins for the Book of Mormon.
Nibley, Hugh. "Lehi in the Desert; the World of the Jaredites; There
  were Jaredites." *The Collected Works of Hugh Nibley,* vol. 4. Salt
  Lake City: Deseret and FARMS, 1988 (repr. of 1952.). The first and
  hugely influential Mormon apologetics that employed cultural and
  textual criticism to argue for the Book of Mormon's plausibility.
Parry, Donald W., Daniel C. Peterson, and John W. Welch. *Echoes and
  Evidences of the Book of Mormon.* Provo, UT: Foundation for
  Ancient Research and Mormon Studies, 2002. A collection of essays

and developments that argue in favor of the Book of Mormon's historicity.

Vogel, Dan, and Brent Lee Metcalfe. *American Apocrypha: Essays on the Book of Mormon*. Salt Lake City: Signature, 2002. Another collection that challenges orthodox understanding of the Book of Mormon's status as an ancient record.

Index

Nebuchadnezzar, 13, 90
Nephi: as abridger/editor, 11, 37; as
    historical character, 7; as son and
    father, 42; as writer, 7, 14, 17, 40, 43,
    62, 63–64, 86; commissioned to keep
    clan history, 4; flees brothers, 43;
    makes plates of ore, 7, 36; on Doctrine
    of Christ, 70; on importance of Isaiah,
    37–38; sees Christ in vision, 18; slays
    Laban, 40
Nephi (chief judge), 57–58
Nephites: and Native Americans, 116;
    anticipate Christ, 71; as Book of
    Mormon audience, 86; civil war
    among, 52; destruction foretold,
    28, 72, 86; institute judges, 54;
    meaning of term, 118; ministered
    to by Lamanites, 56; protect people
    of Ammon, 49; succumb to
    pride cycle, 56; visited by Christ,
    30, 87, 88; warfare with Lamanites,
    51, 56
Neum, 37
New Jerusalem, 125
New Testament, 5, 7, 26, 28, 70, 72, 74,
    91, 106, 107
Nibley, Hugh, 118–20

O

O'Dea, Thomas, 4
olive culture, 119
Oman, 117
Omni, 9, 33, 41, 72, 86–87, 127

P

pacifism, 48
Page, Hiram, 100
Pahoran, 53
Paul, 45, 71
Pearl of Great Price, 107
Pitcairn Island, 40
place names from Book of
    Mormon, 109
plates of brass, 40
Pratt, Orson, 69, 127
Pratt, Parley, 107
pride, 72–73
prisca theologia, 30

provenance: as Book of Mormon theme,
    8, 11, 12, 35
Puritans, 31

Q

qasida, 119

R

Raish, Martin, 117
Red Sea, 90
Reorganized Church of Jesus Christ of
    Latter Day Saints. *See* Community
    of Christ
revelation: in Book of Mormon and Bible
    compared, 15, 17, 20–24; to Joseph
    Smith, 78
Revelation, Book of, 115, 117
Rigdon, Sidney, 114
Ruth, Book of, 60

S

Samuel the Lamanite, 59
San'a, 117
Sariah, 41, 59
Schliemann, Heinrich, 4
Scott, Walter, 70
scripture: as extended memory, 41;
    redefined by Book of Mormon, 41;
    value of, 16, 19, 40
Second Great Awakening, 4
Second Temple, 90
sexual immorality, 72
Skousen, Royal, 128
small plates, 8, 36
Smith, Ethan: *View of the
    Hebrews*, 114
Smith, Hyrum, 101, 126
Smith, Joseph, *91*; Book of Mormon as
    sign of prophetic calling, 123; First
    Vision of, *92*, 129; obtains gold
    plates, 4, *93*; organizes LDS church,
    130; religious principles of, 70, 108;
    revises Book of Mormon, 127;
    translates Book of Mormon,
    94–98; visited by angel Moroni,
    4, 91–92, 129